BONE
BY
BONE

Healing from Preverbal
and Childhood Abuse

You know a book is good when it makes you more aware, when it pauses you to contemplate and question; in this case, to wonder about your own triggers and those of others. The seeds of compassion grow in you. Dawn presents her journey in such a living and authentic way that the invitation to travel with her is easily accepted. She beautifully and courageously models the path of transformation from woundedness to the ever-growing capacity to giving and receiving love and gratitude for the whole of it.

~ Joseph Rubano, father, grandfather, poet, counselor, retreat leader

BONE BY BONE; Healing From Preverbal and Childhood Abuse is an inspiring account of recovery from preverbal, infant and childhood trauma. I was deeply moved by the author's journey as she transforms her suffering into gratitude, forgiveness, and ultimately love, offering readers both hope and illumination.

~ Marla Browning, parent, caregiver, trauma survivor

A courageous and powerful quest born of a desire to restore body and soul to wholeness, *BONE BY BONE Healing from Preverbal and Childhood Abuse* serves as a valuable therapeutic read for anyone who is on a path of recovery from abuse and trauma as well as an informative tool for therapists and other professionals in the field.

~ Mary McMaster, LN, Critical Care Manager, caregiver

A thoughtful reflection on how deep the fissures of childhood trauma can run throughout our lives and within the very core of who we are. Visceral, honest and human, *BONE BY BONE: Healing from Preverbal and Childhood Abuse* is also a powerful account of the journey to bring light into those fissures to realize lasting self-healing.

~ Charles Noyes, nurse practitioner, parent

BONE BY BONE starts out as a moving story of extreme childhood neglect and the trauma it creates, but this isn't simply a book about recovering from childhood trauma. Nelson's healing journey blossoms into an extraordinary flower seldom seen in these sorts of accounts. It's a spiritual, compelling tale about Presence: being with. Presence is Neglect's opposite. Practicing Presence with her children, family, community, in deep inquiry intensives, and with those in Hospice care, Dawn cultivates forgiveness and gratitude and halts the cycle of inter-generational trauma. It is beautiful and inspiring.

~ Cynthia Spillman, artist, parent, coach, trauma survivor

An essential read for therapists who deal with adverse childhood experiences, toxic stress, and trauma. Author Dawn Nelson helps us to heal as she fearlessly delves into the details of her abusive neglect. As we learn from her own course, we can identify our own experiences reflected in her journey, and envision our recovery. For practitioners of the healing arts, *BONE BY BONE* deepens the lens on trauma through the survivor's perspective.

~ Stephan Betz PhD, neurologic music therapist, parent, grandparent, trauma survivor

Dawn Nelson's memoir speaks to me on many levels, both personally and spiritually. Her courage in reliving her early childhood trauma and seeking to both understand and transform her abandonment evokes one's personal—and for most of us—complicated emotions about parenting and family dynamics.

~ Carl Thiermann, parent; retired educator

This incredibly personal and brave book has much to give, revealing how to heal from preverbal and early childhood wounding as the author takes apart her previous narratives and adaptations in an excruciating, bone by bone process.

~ Kathryn Ridall PhD, psychotherapist, author

Not just another trauma story, this book is a deeply personal and powerful narrative that brings new understanding to the growing field of trauma treatment. A survivor of preverbal as well as recurring early childhood abandonment, Dawn Nelson wrote *BONE BY BONE: Healing from Preverbal and Childhood Trauma* tracking the unfoldment of her life and how she ultimately discovered the freedom, strength and creative insights of her true Self.

~ Anna Billings, psychotherapist, life coach, workshop leader

This book is an exploration of trauma, healing and the transformative power of compassion with the eyes and heart of a child, navigating the neglect, abuse and confusion that shaped her early years. Through raw honesty and deep reflection, she helps us understand how we can process childhood trauma, and loss, reminding us that pain and suffering can also have the potential for growth and healing, and that like the lotus rising from the mud, we too can blossom, no matter how difficult our past.

~ Audrey Silverman Foote, LMFT, SEP, parent, grandparent

In a true and authentic voice, author Dawn Nelson tells her story, which is tragic and hopeful, full of raw honesty, courage, wisdom and faith. Dawn took me with her, moment by moment, from her infancy through her transformation to reveal the loving Being that she has always been. She is a living example of how suffering and pain can be healed, and how one can discover the truth of who and what we actually are. I highly recommend *BONE BY BONE* for any individual who wants to know more about healing from trauma.

~ Grace Honore, parent, grandparent, writer, educator, group facilitator, trauma survivor

Other books by Dawn Nelson

Compassionate Touch: Hands on Caregiving for the Elderly,
the Ill and the Dying Station Hill Press, 1994

Die Kraft der heilsamen Berührung
Alte Menschen, Kranke und Sterbende liebevoll umsorgen
Kosel, 1996

Making Friends with Cancer, Findhorn Press, 2000
Freundschaft mit dem Krebs, Ennsthaler Verlag, 2001

From the Heart Through the Hands: The Power of Touch in
Caregiving Findhorn Press, 2001, 2006, 2009

Little Girl Found: How I Reclaimed My Self After Early
Childhood Trauma
Solificatio, SF, California, 2021

BONE
BY
BONE

Healing from Preverbal and Childhood Abuse

DAWN NELSON

Foreword by Lawrence Noyes

solificatio

San Francisco, California

Published by
Solificatio, San Francisco, California
2025

ISBN: 979-8-9858781-6-5

Images of USS Houston in 1938 and of President Roosevelt in his
cabin aboard the USS Houston from the wikimedia.org
free media repository.

Photos in Chapter Ten: Brock Palmer; Barry Barankin

Cover Design by Shelby Putnam Tupper
Interior Design by Carlos Wolters

for all survivors of life-shaping trauma

for parents, grandparents, adoptive and foster parents

counselors, caregivers, therapists, health care professionals

and for the teachers, the helpmates and the healers

Contents

Foreword   xiii

Preface   xv

Terminology   xix

Section One: Seminal Trauma

One: Inception   3

Two: Back Story   5

Three: Illusions Shattered   11

Four: The New (Almost) Mother & Then Another   25

Five: The "Home"   41

Section Two: Life Shaping Psychological Effects

Six: A Few (Nearly) Normal Years   69

Seven: The Phone Call, The Meeting, The Visitation   97

Eight: Ramifications and Reverberations   109

Section Three: Pathways to Healing

Nine: Portals to Awakening   129

Ten: Lessons from the Elderly, the Ill and the Dying   145

Eleven: Forgiving Esther   159

Twelve: Goddess Descending (The Larger Story)   169

Thirteen: Gratitude   175

Fourteen: Blessing Others   181

Fifteen: Forgiveness   187

Appendices

I   Last Visit with Nana   193

II Practicing Gratitude   195

III A Forgiveness Exercise   207

With Gratitude to   211

Suggested Reading   213

Online Resources   217

About the Author   219

Index   221

Foreword

I first met Dawn over forty years ago, during the time she writes about in the chapter entitled "Portals to Awakening" in *BONE BY BONE Healing from Preverbal and Childhood Abuse*, and I witnessed the deeper parts of her inner search begin to flower. She was curious about who she really is and was deeply committed to diving into that mystery using any method that held promise.

Dawn's journey led her to more than just a healing for herself. It awakened in her a new life purpose of serving the elderly, the ill, and the dying through the therapeutic model of skilled touch that she created and eventually taught to others. It led to something great coming through her and breaking new ground in the field of compassionate caregiving for those often marginalized groups of individuals. This unsought consequence of her search emerges from her narrative unexpectedly and, for me, validates her efforts even more.

This unique memoir offers the reader useful insights into the various ways in which Dawn's developmental abuse and the repeated physical and emotional abandonment she endured in her early life influenced her thinking and colored her choices in adulthood. The book details the ways in which her life changed after she gave up wishing that her infancy and childhood had been different, ultimately turning the adversity she experienced in childhood into a blessing. *BONE BY BONE* is a compelling and inspirational memoir detailing a valiant journey which is, in many ways, all our journeys. It is about the search for our true selves.

~ Lawrence Noyes, author, educator, parent, grandparent
Santa Fe, New Mexico

Preface

Perhaps there was no more detrimental consequence of our childhood abandonment than being forced to hide our authentic selves.

~ Pete Walker

The paradox of trauma is that it has both the power to destroy and the power to transform.

~ Peter A. Levine

BONE BY BONE is a revision/expansion of *Little Girl Found: How I Reclaimed My Self After Early Childhood Trauma (2021)*. That offering was the result of a long endeavor to examine and process my early memories, along with information gathered from primary sources, regarding my serial neglect and abandonment as an infant and subsequent traumatic emotional and psychological abuse during my childhood.

Opening to memories from both physical and emotional abandonments I experienced in my childhood was revelatory. It became increasingly obvious that those events had shaped my personality and had influenced my habits, attitudes, decisions, and behaviors well into adulthood. Embracing and reframing those memories through writing about them, as well as seeing them through the lens of my present perspective, helped me release the residual trauma in my body, brain, and psyche. It allowed me to forgive others and myself, and increased my compassion for us all.

I continue to notice ways in which that developmental wounding affected my cognitive abilities and thinking patterns as well as my attention span and how it colored many of my choices in later life. My attachment to others' approval can still arise from a casual comment or tone of voice from a loved one. To this day, I sometimes feel myself falling into a long-held habit of adapting to what I perceive others want rather than making conscious decisions for myself. I'm nearly always "triggered" by the sound of a wailing baby. I recognize personal patterns and habits—both negative and positive—that can be traced to the lack of physical contact and neglect in my infancy as well as to the intermittent physical and emotional neglect during my childhood. I've come to understand why repeated abandonment experiences can create toxic shame and why touch is so essential to infants.

Noted Swiss author and Psychologist, Alice Miller said that "The structuring of the brain depends very much on events experienced in the first hours, days and weeks of a person's life." The persistent absence of responsive care disrupts the developing brain, the amygdala in particular, "the part of the limbic system that plays a key role in the processing of emotions and memories that have to do with fear." (developingchild.harvard.edu). Some researchers postulate that just as postpartum depression can interfere with bonding, childhood trauma can begin in utero if a mother is highly stressed, and can affect a mother's ability to bond with her baby.

The various types of maltreatment that I and countless others have experienced have now been researched, named, and delineated by psychologists and experts in their fields: ACS (Abandoned Child Syndrome); ACE (Adverse Childhood Experiences); AD (Attachment Disorder); ASCA (Adult Survivors of Childhood Abuse); CEN (Childhood Emotional Neglect); CPDSD (Complex Post Traumatic Stress Syndrome); DTD (Developmental Trauma Disorder); RT (Relational Trauma) and so on. Studies are revealing ways in which how we are cared for before birth, as infants, and as children have a crucial impact on how we will view ourselves and relate to others as we age.

There is now increasing support available from mental health professionals, therapists and researchers specializing in trauma-informed modalities. We can access online healing trauma summits, and talks with physicians, psychiatrists, and researchers. There are any number of podcasts and YouTube talks as well as books by psychologists, and meditation and mindfulness teachers as well as a growing number of personal narratives by trauma survivors.

Sharing our stories is a crucial part of how we help each other heal. May you find something in my journey that will support you in your own or that may increase your understanding of what someone you love may be struggling with. May we move beyond our assumptions, and the labels we've attached to ourselves and to others. May we relinquish self-defeating thoughts and self judgements. May we all find ways to release the wounds of the past, and to let go of what we cannot change in order to embrace our true selves and each other in the here and now.

There is a light in the bones a sacred hollow, vast and light, where we are always standing. ~ Joseph Rubano

Dawn Nelson
July, 2025
Walnut Creek, CA

Terminology

The words listed below are defined according to their usage within the context of this book.

Abandoned: left alone; neglected; rejected; relinquished.

Abuse: behaviors that harm a child's self-worth, including physical, verbal, or emotional mistreatment.

Developmental Trauma: used to describe childhood trauma including physical, emotional or psychological; abandonment or rejection by a primary caregiver while the brain is still growing and changing.

Dissociation: an experience in which an individual feels detached from thoughts or feelings; becoming disconnected from any sense of self, going numb, blanking out, shutting down mentally and emotionally.

Forgiveness: letting go of judgements, blame and negative feelings towards another or towards oneself.

Healing: resolving; making peace with one's past; coming to terms with things as they are.

Mindfulness: conscious, intentional awareness; being fully present and focused; paying attention; open to each moment without judgement.

Neglect: the absence of attention, responsiveness, and protection appropriate to the needs of an infant or child; physical or emotional absence; disregard.

Spiritual: relating to the human spirit; involving a search for meaning, something intangible, sacred, divine.

Trauma: from the Greek meaning wounding; life-changing wounds–physical, emotional, verbal, sexual, and/or psychological that lead to disconnection, confusion, anxiety, depression, or despair; the result of events or circumstances experienced by an individual as harmful or threatening and which have lasting adverse effects on well-being.

A Guide to How Voices in This Book are Differentiated

1. Narration: plain text

2. Direct Quotes: indented or in quotation marks

3. Memories: indented and bolded

4. Current perspectives: italics

MOTHER PLACED UNDER SUSPENDED JAIL SENTENCE headlines the article on the front page of the *KENTUCKY TIMES-STAR* for Thursday, September 14, 1944. The news story states that the 24-year-old mother was given a jail sentence of 30 days when she pleaded guilty to a charge of neglecting her 13-month-old daughter. The County juvenile officer is quoted as saying she had received numerous complaints about the alleged failure of the mother in caring for the child, leaving the child alone in the home, going out and coming back at a late hour . . . The Judge ordered the child placed in the custody of her paternal grandparents pending a further order from the court and severely reprimanded the young mother. The article ends by stating that "the child has been in Speers Hospital since early last Sunday, and that the father has not seen his daughter."

That child was me . . .

Section One

Seminal Trauma

One

Inception

Write what disturbs you, what you fear, what you have not been willing to speak about. Be willing to be split open.
~ Natalie Goldberg

Your anger and damage and grief are the way to truth . . .
~ Anne Lamont

My three children were flourishing as adults and I was blessed with several grandchildren before I was led to re-visit the narrative I had long held in regard to my birth, first year of life and early childhood. Extensive biological and developmental research has now shown that consequential neglect—the ongoing disruption or significant absence of caregiver responsiveness—can cause more harm to a young child's development than overt physical abuse. Neuroscientists have learned that the most crucial stage for brain development is the first year of life.

I truly thought I had dealt with my abandonment issues during countless hours of cognitive and somatic therapy sessions, and through engaging in various meditative practices. As new evidence of my biological mother's persistent neglect in my first thirteen months of life was revealed, and I began recognizing and remembering subsequent abandonments, I thought I might drown in the sea of sorrow that began to engulf me. I wondered if I could survive experiencing the long- denied pain of the wounding, much less the anger that I would eventually realize was smoldering beneath.

Perhaps poet Emily Dickinson was correct when she wrote

> There is a pain—so utter—
> It swallows substance up—

Perhaps there are traumatic wounds so completely unrecognizable and untenable to an infant that the being is swallowed up. The individual disappears inside the agony of not being seen, of not being heard, of not being valued, of not being wanted. With nobody to mirror reality, that small being shapes a mask from whatever models may (or may not) be nearby and eventually creates a persona to go with it, develops a story, a belief system such as "I'm not good enough" or "I don't deserve to be loved."

> Then covers the Abyss with Trance—
> So memory can step
> Around—across—upon it

The child falls asleep to it's true nature and forgets that which the mind cannot yet comprehend, in order to survive.

> As one within a Swoon—
> Goes safely—where an open eye—
> Would drop Him—Bone by Bone.

Wrapped in the cocoon of forgetfulness, the growing child can feel safe and protected, can perhaps forgo fully experiencing the pain of separation and rejection, thus averting a slow and agonizing fall into a chasm of darkness. Eventually, however, the longing for Self prevails. There comes a time when it is no longer possible to avoid the Abyss, when there is nowhere else to go, when there is nothing else to do but to face the demons who lurk in the darkness that blocks out the light of knowing.

Two

Back Story

We all are the continuation of our fathers, our mothers, our ancestors.
~ Thich Nhat Hanh

A mother is a child's first looking glass into the world
~ Rachelle E. Goodrich

The man who would become my father was a precocious musician from a young age. In 1936-37, while still in high school, he was playing in a Cincinnati, Ohio ballroom and getting other jobs through the musicians' union when his father heard about a new Naval program in Washington DC for musicians. He advised his son to apply. Years later, during an interview with my dad that had begun with a casual question I'd asked about his musical history, he recounted what had occurred next:

> Ken: So, I went to DC to try out for the program. There was a big deal made of this in the local papers and all about my appointment, and my picture was in the paper and everything. And it gave me a swelled head, to the extent that when they announced I'd made it, I couldn't very well say I didn't want it.

> Dawn: You didn't really want to go? Why not?

> Ken: It was the adulation that made me go. And the training was virtually nothing. They simply didn't give you what they said in writing they would. It was supposed to be similar to going to Juilliard or the Cincinnati School of Music or some comparable place

where you would receive intensive musical Training. But that wasn't what it turned out to be. It was more like basic training with a service organization, including training on how to survive as a navy man. There was almost no musical training at all and that wasn't what I'd signed up for.

As it turned out, fate, and perhaps his own resolve, intervened and my father was able to escape the situation he had unhappily found himself in at that point in his life.

Ken: There were some people there who already knew about my dislike of the whole set up and these guys were due to graduate. They had already formed a band and just needed a good clarinet and sax man get assigned to their unit so they went to the guy in charge of bands and told him their situation and he made an exception.

The band my father managed to join played at the 1939 World's Fair in New York City for six months before boarding the  USS Phoenix for their "shakedown cruise," (testing phase of a new watercraft) which covered the entire east coast of South America and the Panama Canal before returning to the Florida coast, and disembarking in South Carolina. The band was then transferred to the USS Houston (a Northampton-class heavy cruiser commissioned in 1930, and sunk in 1942). The USS Houston was said to be FDR's favorite when he was surveying the fleet, presiding over mock battles, or sometimes just going deep sea fishing. My father kept an informative and descriptive handwritten diary from Dec. 22, 1938 – March 22, 1939 in a little leather book with gilt-edged pages. Part of the entry dated February 21, 1939. reads, "Had a rehearsal and played a concert at noon. Then watched the President and party go out fishing. F.D.R. looks fine, all but his legs—they're a pitiful sight. He does no walking whatsoever." Elsewhere, he describes what occurred when the President wanted to go fishing. "They

FDR in his cabin on the USS Houston

lowered a dinghy over the side of the ship and he would be gone half a day and then come back and show his catch to anyone who wanted to view it. The band played each time he came back on board." If no fish were caught the band did not have to play colors.

After being discharged from the navy, my father was looking for work in Los Angeles in order to get his musician's union card when he received a letter advising him to report for induction into the US Army. Unlike other young men of his time, or so we are given to believe, my father admitted towards the end of his life that he hadn't actually considered being in the military an especially honorable obligation or a heroic pursuit. He did add that he was really "anti-regiment" as well as "pretty cocky" at that time of his life.

> Ken: I was convinced that I would go in there and tell them I'd been in the navy and they'd say, "We can't use you!" But they said Health—A-OK. I argued with the sergeant and even went to the chaplain, but the next day I was on the troop train going to Fort Benning, Georgia.

According to my father he met the woman who would give birth to me at Daytona Beach, Florida while on a weekend pass: "Just like all the other soldiers, out for a good time." I imagine she was one among other young women also looking for "a good time" with a soldier. A twenty-one-year-old divorcee, the woman my father spent time with that day called herself Penny. It is unclear exactly how many days or hours she and my father actually spent in each other's physical company prior to their marriage, which took place in Fort Thomas, Kentucky December 14, 1941. The faded newspaper clipping announcing the marriage says the groom was on a fifteen-day furlough, and that the bride was "wearing a wool frock and a gardenia  corsate." The last line of the announcement mentions that "the couple will pass the next week at the home of the groom's parents before moving into their apartment in Baker Village at Fort Benning."

Nearly fifty years later, during an afternoon of recorded reminiscing with his two sisters, my father recalls being "shipped out" with the 2nd Armored Division of the US Army, about a year after his wedding, in December of 1942. His younger sister, Bobbie, then asked a question about where Penny went when he shipped overseas, which generated the following dialogue:

> Ken: Oh, she went back to her mother in Daytona. When she found out that she was pregnant, she came to Fort. Thomas to stay with the folks.
>
> Bobbie: Was that her idea?
>
> Ken: I think it was Mom's . . . I'm not sure.
>
> Bobbie: You'd think she'd want to be with her own mother.
>
> Ken: Oh, not **her** mother! That was Penny's **problem**, her Mother!

This rather vehement declaration by my father in regard to his first mother-in-law is not elaborated on, although there were other hints here and there that would lead one to believe she was a fairly narcissistic and manipulative woman, as well as a heavy drinker. It is quite likely that she was an alcoholic, as her only daughter would become, given that both genes and environment are known to play a role in that particular addiction.

In a recorded conversation about six months before his death, I asked my father if he knew Penny was pregnant before he left to go overseas.

Ken: No. She told me in a letter.

Dawn: How did you feel when you got that news?

Ken: I was very, very pleased.

I do wish I had thought to ask my father at that time if his then wife had shared any thoughts regarding how she felt about being pregnant or about the prospect of giving birth. I also failed to find out if they had been hoping that she would get pregnant before he went overseas. He didn't recall being consulted about names, saying he was "taken aback" when he was told she chose the name Dawn because it was so unusual. Information beyond my birth certificate concerning my actual entrance into this world is scarce.

My father shared that he did remember Penny saying in a letter, "There is no way I'm going to give birth without drugs." She moved out of my grandparents' house shortly after my birth into her own apartment. The two-story red brick structure in Fort. Thomas, Kentucky, still pictured on the internet, was built in 1927 and last sold in 2007. It the photo, the building seems to consist of five units. It is quite obvious in statements Penny makes about my grandmother in her letters to my father during the following months that she valued her own independence and ideas more than any help or advice that might be offered by the mother of her husband, who had successfully raised three children.

My father's draft into the Army was for one year, although, as he explained

> . . . but then the war came two months before my option was up and until the war was over, there was no option. I asked for an emergency leave when you were born, and it finally came through almost two years later!

I was eighteen months old when I actually laid eyes on my father in person for a short time before he returned to the service. By that time, my mother had been declared unfit to care for me, and I had been in my grandparents' custody for five months.

Three

Illusions Shattered

*In order to grow from an experience, we first have to acknowledge
an experience. This is particularly true in the case of trauma.*
~ Steve Taylor

*Disconnection from the Self is the first thing that happens in trauma . . .
the greatest calamity wasn't that there was no longer support but that you
lost connection to your Essence.*
~ Gabor Maté

When the large envelope from the Kentucky Department for Libraries
and Archives arrives, it is thicker than I expected. I hesitate before
opening it, surprised by the trickle of trepidation I'm feeling, along
with my eagerness to search the contents. Inside the envelope I find
twenty-five pages of copied legal documents, along with the divorce
decree releasing my father from the bonds of matrimony with Grace
Elise Armor (the woman known as Penny) date stamped April 25,
1945. There are three legal depositions: one with my father, Kenneth
C. Armor; one with my grandfather, Claude A. Amor; and one with
Laurel Lyons, probation officer. At the time the depositions were
taken, my father had been in the US Army over four years, overseas
for two and a half of those.

    The longest deposition is with my father and I read it first. After
a few identifying, preliminary questions, the examining lawyer asks if
he heard from his wife regularly while he was overseas, and my father
answers: "Not after the first year." Attorney Scott then directs him
to read a salient paragraph or two from a letter he received from his
wife, dated June 21, 1944.

I didn't think I would ever come to the point of asking you what am about to while you were overseas, thinking it would be kinder to wait until you returned. However, you seem to be doing a lot of planning for the future and I don't feel that we have one together. I have met someone with whom I am very much in love and want nothing more than to spend the rest of my life with him. I would be willing to do the right thing about the baby, that is let you see or have her as often as the Court ordained.

Was she drunk when she wrote that! Delusional? Was she simply using me as a pawn to manipulate my father? Did she think of me as a possession? How did my father feel as he was reading her words? Was he saddened? Angry? Depressed?

Although it was not referred to in the court proceedings that day, I possess another hand-written letter from Penny to my father, dated less than two weeks later, July 9, 1944. In a long, rambling message she tells my father, among a number of other complaints, to "tell your mother she does not have to feel responsible for my welfare in any way any longer. I would rather be left alone." She then says that she thinks her last letter to him was written because she was feeling lonely and vulnerable, followed by the sentence: "If we get back together, I think I could love you almost as much as I once did, but I would prefer that you make the decision." She then adds

There is one job I have been working at for the last eleven months that your mother or anyone else cannot say I have failed at and that is the raising of my child. I feel if we separate, I am entitled to the baby since I have done it all by myself. I'm sure you will agree.

Perusing these words again, more than sixty years after they were penned, juxtaposed with the depositions I had in front of me was unnerving. It awakened both shock and compassion in me, along with multiple questions.

Did Penny actually believe what was she saying? Is this type of thinking caused by what is referred to as alcoholic brain? Were the words she was writing a cunning attempt to control or to somehow punish my father? How irrational was she? Was she suffering from a mental disorder or perhaps a bad case of post-partum depression? Or was it simply classic narcissism?

The attorney continues questioning my father:

> Q: You know now, since your return, that your wife apparently has no interest in the child is that correct?

> A: Yes, only a selfish interest, that is to want to possess her without sharing any responsibility.

No interest in the child! Can that really be true? Did she ever feel any emotional attachment to me at all? I am hit by a wave of anger, grief, and sadness—for me, for my father and for the woman who brought me into the world yet who was apparently unable to accept, love, embrace, or see me as anything but an inconvenience. My mouth suddenly opens up and out and I hear a protracted, piercing AAAAAAAAAHHHHHHHH sound bursting forth before hissing and growling sounds emerge. I feel my face morph into some kind of cat-like creature with teeth bared defensively. My hands rise upwards to the sides of my face, my fingers curling like an angry house cat or wildcat about to strike . . .

The next part of my father's deposition concerns the amount of money Penny was receiving monthly at that time: $150.00 from her Guardian—income from a trust fund left to her by her biological father—in addition to a governmental allotment of $80 per month once I was born. My father adds that before my birth, "She received an average of $130.00 a month" from him. A quick bit of research tells me that the total sum of money she had at her disposal after my arrival was more than the average wage for all occupations in 1943.

If Penny didn't want to call on my grandparents for babysitting relief, why wouldn't she have hired help of some kind when she clearly had enough money to do so? Why wouldn't she have offered to pay a neighbor in her apartment building to look after me when she wanted to go out or have a little time to herself? What kept her from asking a neighbor to at least check on me occasionally, when she left me alone in the apartment, while I was presumably sleeping?

As the questioning continues, my father reports that upon his arrival in Fort Thomas on the leave which was finally granted, he spent a few days with me and his parents before he then took me "to the residence his wife had established for herself, in order to try and work things out with her."

> Q: Why did you take the child back to your parent's home?
>
> A: Because my wife would not take care of the child, and also because she requested that I do that. that I do that.
>
> Q: What is her attitude toward this child of hers and yours?
>
> A: She's quite frank about it. Saying she does not want the child to interfere with her personal life.

My father goes on to describe the specific event that persuaded him that "this was not going to work out." My wife had asked me if I wanted to stay in a picture show this particular evening, and she would take care of the child, she would take her home. When I came out of the show, I found her in the corner cafe drinking beer, and she was with two soldiers. I asked her if she would like to go to the show and I would take care of the baby. She said she would. That night she came in about 12:30 a.m. rather drunk which of course meant that the next morning, she had to get over the night before.

My emotions are roiling. I feel as if I am flotsam riding the waves of a raging sea crashing against a rocky shore. Exhausted and unsettled by the words I am reading, yet engrossed, I press on in pursuit of details surrounding this critical part of my infancy. Recognizing the name Laurel Lyons as the Probation Officer quoted in the now yellowed newspaper clipping about my birth mother's arrest, I turn to her deposition. Once her history, seven and a half years as Probation Officer for Campbell County, and connection with the case are established, Ms. Lyons is asked to "recite what you know of Mrs. Armor's attitude and conduct toward her child." Ms. Lyons days that she'd received a number of complaints from neighbors in the building and in the neighborhood about a Mrs. Penny Armor "neglecting the baby, leaving the baby alone day and night whenever she went out."

> Many times, when Mrs. Armor would be out in the afternoon different friends would ask her where the baby was, and many times the baby was home where there was never anyone to attend to it. . . Another lady that lived in the building said that if Mrs. Armor took a notion to go out, if only she would just have left the door open, so that they could have gotten to the baby if anything had happened. Another neighbor had said that Penny would be out all night many nights. The next day it was necessary to sleep all day and the baby was just in the apartment without any attention.

And just like that I am yanked out of my illusions. I can no longer protect myself by even pretending to believe the story I often hoped might be true: my birth mother was inexperienced, depressed, tired, and terribly lonely. She left me alone after I went to sleep at night a few times to have a drink at a nearby bar. One night she had too much to drink, met someone who took advantage of her loneliness, someone who had no idea she'd left a sleeping baby alone in an apartment. He took her to his place to sleep it off and she was so exhausted she didn't wake up for a night and a day, or maybe she woke in such a confused state that she somehow just let herself momentarily forget about her baby. I must accept the fact that the woman whose physical body afforded me passage into this world wasn't just unprepared for or overwhelmed by motherhood, she was actually unwilling, or unable, to accept that role, to bond with me or to put caring for me above her own desires and addictions. Her neglect was chronic and ongoing. I was an inconvenience. I wasn't valued. I wasn't important. I wasn't embraced. I wasn't claimed. I was left unattended repeatedly, uncared for and, essentially, unmothered during the entire first year of my life.

If there were numerous complaints, why wasn't some action taken sooner? What was it that compelled Ms. Lyons to act so quickly on that particular autumn evening? What was different that time? Had the same person called previously? And what caused her, or him, to call at that specific time and hour? Anger? Frustration? Concern or compassion for me?

My mind jumps back to the summer of my twelfth birthday when my beloved grandparents were visiting for a week or two. One day Nana took me to a department store and led me to the section where there were dozens of colors of nail polish. I was surprised and thrilled when she told me to pick out any color I wanted, and that she would also buy me a tube of lipstick to match it. I chose a deep pink labeled "True Love." After we got back to the house, she taught me how to paint my fingernails, although I never really developed a propensity for that particular embellishment. The real gift that day was the time we spent together, my grandmother's hugs, and her acknowledgement that I was "growing up." The next day, she and my father asked me to sit down with them on the sofa facing the big picture window in the new three-bedroom brick house where my father, my stepmother Ruth Ann, and I were living.

> **Daddy is perched on the arm of our living room sofa. I am sitting between him and Nana, who is saying that she thinks I am old enough to know what they are about to tell me. Nana glances at my father before speaking: When you were just over one year old, your mother left you alone for three days and nights. The police came and rescued you and you were taken to the hospital for a few days, and after that you came to live with us.' She smiles and squeezes my hand. I smile back and return her squeeze.**

The deeper significance of my grandmother's words fell on deaf ears, one might say—at the time—either because my mind was preoccupied with pre-teen fantasies or, possibly, because I wasn't ready to cope with such a revelation. I don't recall even asking any questions. After Nana said her piece, my father handed me a large envelope with a file folder inside, telling me I should save the information, keep the documents safe, and look through them whenever I was ready to do so. It would be a couple of years before I gave them more than a cursory read-through and a couple of decades before I would peruse them in any depth before setting them aside once again.

I return to Ms. Lyon's testimony, and continue reading her testimony.

> We were unable to rouse anyone upon our arrival at the home. We then entered the apartment through the living room window.

The police must surely have knocked several times on the door, perhaps loudly, before deciding to come in through a window which seems to have been on the first floor of the two-story building and which they were able to open without breaking the glass. Had others already knocked on the door? Do I have some preverbal sense memory from that time that is responsible for my sensitivity to loud noises, especially in the middle of the night when I occasionally wake up, startled and anxious, wondering if I've dreamed the distinctive door knocking sounds I heard or if they were ever possibly real?

Ms. Lyons then details the disarray that greeted them once they were inside the apartment including dirty dishes on the table and counters, uneaten food in pots and pans on the stove, an empty beer jug, remains of other alcoholic drinks, an unmade bed, a messy bathroom, and so on.

> It looked as if there might have been a party there and they just left it that way. We walked into the bedroom where the baby was in bed. She was awake, and there were two other glasses there, each one was filled with a highball. I proceeded to take the baby out of the bed and look for clothes for her.

More questions vie for my attention. I presume Ms. Lyons needed to find clothing for me because whatever I was wearing, along with the crib mattress and the coverings, were wet and most likely soiled. Why, I wonder, did she mention the two highball glasses near my bed?

Was the door to the bedroom she found me open or closed? Was I able to hear noises from the street or from the other apartments in the building? Was there a window in the bedroom near my crib? Was there a light left on anywhere in the apartment? Could the condition I was found in have anything to do with my lifelong aversion to being cold, with my chronic constipation long into adulthood, with my fear of being alone in the dark? Is there a chance that my lifetime distaste for alcohol in all forms could be related to alcohol being added to whatever was in my bottle or to the constant smell of alcohol around me in the space?

I notice that I am never mentioned by name in the deposition. I am always referred to as "the infant," "the baby," "the child," or even as "it." Ms. Lyons goes on with her account of the night in question: "I took the baby from there and placed it in Speers Hospital. In other words, the baby would have been alone all that night unless I had taken her." She goes on to say that she left the warrant with the policemen "who waited until a car pulled up at about 4:30 a.m.

Tears spring to my eyes as a question I've often pondered is answered. I feel a rush of gratitude for this young woman with the alliterative name now etched in my mind, for her care and compassion that September night so long ago. I experience a wave of immense relief at being discovered, noticed, touched, rescued from the darkness.

The attorney continues questioning Ms. Lyons:

> Q: What was Penny Armor's plea to the charge in
>   the County Court?
>
> A: Guilty.
>
> Q: What did Judge Bertelsman do with respect to
>   custody of the child?
>
> A: He gave the custody to the grandmother.

And so I learn the name of the Judge who, in my grandmother's recounting of this moment when I asked her about it a number of years later, answered, "The Judge said to your mother, 'Do you understand that you are relinquishing all rights to this child from this day forward?'" My grandmother said, "Penny replied, 'yes' and the Judge then instructed her to hand you to me."

Was I awake in that moment? Did I have a bottle, a toy or a blanket that I was holding onto as the transfer was made? What was the woman who had given birth to me experiencing as she handed me to my grandmother?

Did she hesitate, shed any tears? Did she feel any distress or remorse, or was she simply relieved to relinquish the responsibilities she seemed unable to accept? Is it possible that she was actually conscious of the fact that she wasn't able to mother me properly and in complying with the judge's instructions felt that she was giving me up so I would have a better life? I was thirteen months old. What was I sensing or experiencing as the transfer was made?

Toward the end of Ms. Lyon's deposition, I learn that part of the Court's order that day was that Penny would be allowed to visit me at my Grandparents' home if she so chose, "though she did not make her visits very often," Ms. Lyons added.

Q: You continued your investigation to find out
   what her attitude was toward the child?

A: Yes. I just could not see that there was any
   motherly love there at all for the baby that
   is abnormal.

I gasp for breath as I cradle myself with my arms. I begin speaking to that small child that lives inside me, "You are okay now, you're alive. We survived, we are safe, we are loved." My body rocks forwards and backwards. A tsunami of tears cascades like a waterfall over my face, dripping off my chin and wetting my clothing as I give myself permission, at long last, to acknowledge the despair, to mourn for that part of me that was left isolated, alone, crying, hungry, confused. My teeth begin to chatter. I am shivering. I manage to leave my computer chair and stumble to the nearest bed where I turn onto my side and curl up into a fetal position. Unfamiliar, high-pitched sounds are coming out of my throat. I cannot stop them. My eyes are closed. I am gulping air. Eventually, my sobs begin to subside and my tear-stained skin dries. My shivering starts to abate. As I open my eyes to sunlight blanketing the bed and welcome its warmth, my breathing normalizes. I listen to the silence while gazing out the window at fluffy-topped white clouds moving slowly across a beautiful azure sky. A red-tailed hawk with an enormous wing span soars through the air, then tips its wings, and swoops below the clouds disappearing from sight. I breathe deeply blowing air out between my lips and gradually return to my adult body.

Sitting at my desk a few hours later, I finish reading Ms. Lyon's deposition. When she is questioned about her follow-up visits to the home of my grandparents and is asked what kind of home it was, Ms. Lyons answers, "It is just lovely, a real home." When asked if the child was receiving proper attention during her visit, she responded, "It certainly was." At that point, the Probation Officer's deposition ends with a final question from the attorney.

Q: You feel like the custody of that child should
     remain with its grandparents?

A: Yes, I do.

The shortest deposition is with my father's father, whom I called

Granny. His answers to the questions asked of him are straightforward, succinct and without embellishment just as I remember he himself being in later years. I experience a rush of gratitude for my grandfather as I think about his quiet, gentle strength and how protected I felt in his arms, based on memories of him from my very early and later childhood and from photographs my grandmother saved and passed on to me. One unphotographed experience involving him remains embedded in my memory.

**Nana buys me a big red balloon that floats
in the air. I am carrying it proudly, tied
around my right wrist as we walk to the
house. I'm excited to show this wonderful
new thing to Granny. Nana is behind me,
holding onto my left hand, helping me as I
slowly navigate the wooden steps into the
basement where Granny is at his work bench
a few feet away along the right wall. The
balloon bursts suddenly bursts and I break
into tears, frightened by the unexpected loud
noise and broken hearted by the loss of my
most wonderful gift. Granny comes quickly
to the stairs. He doesn't speak. He just lifts
me down and holds me until I stop crying.**

My grandfather's testimony includes the fact that Penny lived
just "a little over a mile away," saying that "it was a short streetcar
ride to within two blocks" of where they lived. He states that the
court had sanctioned visits to me, after they took me into their home.

He said such visits occurred every
couple of weeks in the beginning
"but became less and less frequent,
usually lasting only a half hour or
less." When questioned about his
daughter-in-law's attitude toward
the child my grandfather responds,
"She showed no particular interest
during her visits." This seems to
help explain why, in the earliest
photograph that exists of me
with Penny, clearly taken at my
grandparents' house, during one
of the visits my grandfather describes as being short and increasingly
infrequent. I am not touching her in any way. I am looking at her as
if I don't know who she is, and even seem to be a bit wary of her.

My grandfather is asked if there was any "other activity that would indicate Penny did not want to be burdened with the child." He answers that "she had her phone number removed from listings and would not give it to us." The words of Ms. Lyons, my father, and my grandfather swim and circle in my head like feathers in a breeze:

"no maternal instincts"

"no motherly love at all for the baby"

"complete disregard for any motherly duties"

"didn't want to be burdened"

"unnatural"

"not normal"

"appeared to have no interest in the child"

"doesn't want the child to interfere with her own personal life"

Unexpectedly, I recall my grandmother's answer to a question I once asked her—after experiencing labor and childbirth twice myself—about what my birth had been like for my mother. "She considered it a long, painful and ultimately disappointing ordeal when she didn't see the boy she was hoping for." I let the words she said sink in and rest in my consciousness now in a way that I didn't when my grandmother uttered them.

Is it possible my birth mother might have behaved differently if I had been a boy? Was she unable to love me just because I came into this life in a female body?

Struggling to keep my heart and mind open, I surrender to the revelations of the collective depositions. I feel a lump in my throat extending downward. My chest tightens as my body shakes with quiet sobs until I take a large gulp of air and, without warning, a shrill wail emerges from somewhere deep in my being. I feel the pain of every infant who has ever cried for a mother, a father, or a caregiver who didn't answer, for every child who has ever been left alone, ignored, forgotten, mistreated, rejected, neglected, abandoned. I weep for all the babies and toddlers who weren't rescued, who weren't taken in by loving relatives as I was for a time. I weep for children everywhere who are at this very moment being exploited, misused, and abused in unimaginable and horrific ways, for the children of all ages who are suffering ongoing, unspeakable trauma. I let my heart break open and bleed.

Four

The New (Almost) Mother and Then Another

Traumatic experiences leave traces o our minds and emotions,
and on our capacity for joy and intimacy . . .
~ Bessel Van Der Kolk

The crucial aspect of abuse is not what occurred
but what impact it had on you, how you explained it to yourself
. . . and how it has affected your life.
~ Eliana Gil, Ph.D

During a reorganizing binge shortly after my youngest child is safely settled in college in another state, I come across a collection of oversized negatives in an envelope inside a small box, along with a few black and white photos of my father taken during WWII. Examining the negatives closely I see one with three people: a man, a woman and a young child. I think it likely that the man is my father and the child is me. I am curious enough about the woman to track

 down a place that will print negatives from the 1940s. Peering at the printed photograph, I see my father looking ever so slightly smug, with me sitting on his shoulders, a thin-lipped smile on my face. My father and I are both looking at the person taking the picture, presumably my grandmother. I suddenly realize that the woman in the photograph, is the seldom mentioned Ginger. My father's new bride is looking up at me, a bit dubiously it seems to me. Perhaps she is wondering what she has gotten herself into with this quick marriage that comes with a little girl, not yet two years old, whom she is just

now meeting for the first time? As I study Ginger's face and puzzle over demeanor, I suddenly burst into tears. I hear myself nearly shout, "We could have been a **family**!"

*Why didn't you think a little harder before marrying somebody with such a young child before you'd even met her? Did you even **want** to be a mother? What did I do to drive you away? Was it the bed wetting? The recurrent bronchitis I've been told I already had by that time in my life? How quickly did it dawn on you that you'd made a mistake? Did anyone caution you to think twice before you accepted such a hasty proposal?*

When my husband walks into the room and asks who I am yelling at, I show him the picture of the threesome and explain who Ginger is. He sees something in the image I seem to have missed, remarking, "Nobody in that photo is really claiming you—not your father or this lady he married so hastily." He then points to another photo I've developed, one of me with my father's mother. Studying the image, he says to me, "You can  feel the love in this photograph he says. You can see that this person is claiming you. She's watching over you and she is loving you. This woman is saying, 'I've got your back. I'm here for you no matter what.'"

My tears flow even faster. Remembering the unconditional love that I received from my grandmother, I am flooded with emotion, wonderstruck as I reflect on the commitment and the sacrifices my grandparents made by taking me into their home and caring for me at that stage in my life and in theirs. I am becoming increasingly aware of the deep significance of their responsive love and devotion. It most surely interrupted and counterbalanced the cycle of repeated neglect and distress in my infancy, and it undoubtedly saved me from what would have most likely been far more serious consequences in my development going forward.

Searching for what my father said about his second wife in the interviews I conducted with him in 1989, I locate the section where he is remembering his release from the Army. He said he had been sent to Ft. Ord, on the Central California coast, until the war was over and, after that, to Camp Beale Air Force Base for discharge. The Army then paid for his flight to Los Angeles since that's where he'd been living when inducted. He was looking for work in LA when he received a wire from his roommate from the Army, drummer Tom Dribble:

> He wanted to know if I'd want a job with Lloyd LaBrie who was going on the road to see if he could make it. was tickled to death to hear from somebody that I knew and to get work so I said yes. The band was on the way to Kansas City and I joined them there . . . I met Ginger in Kansas City and then the band was playing in Youngstown, Ohio and I called her up and said, "How'd you like to get married?" She said OK and she flew up to Youngstown, and we got married.

Whoa! What? Who does such a thing? What were you thinking? What was she thinking? Did you tell her about me before or after you asked her to marry you? Did she ask any questions about me? Did you show her a picture of me and she said I was cute? Did either of you have a clue about what being a parent actually requires?!

Thirty-eight years have passed since I transcribed my father's words. When I heard them, instead of probing further on how she might have reacted when his new wife met me, all I said to him was, "Kind of a short courtship!" Then, instead of asking the obvious questions, I merely said, "And then what?"

Ken:
I left the band then and went to Cincinnati . . . we stayed with the folks and I got jobs easily. After about three months, Ginger decided she wasn't a mother and took off to Kansas City on the pretext of visiting an aunt, or sister, but really, she was leaving me. She later wrote and asked for money to get a divorce. It was really kind of devious because she had already gotten the divorce. I wrote to the Kansas Courts to see if she'd filed for divorce. They wrote back and said that, yes, she was divorced.

Dawn:
What! You mean she could get a divorce without you even knowing it?

Ken:
Oh, yeah they would just say she was abandoned. I wasn't around so it was abandonment and why look any further into the matter?

Dawn:
Were you upset? I mean did you really love her?

Ken:
I suppose I loved her at the time but it wasn't a really deep love. To be honest it was a marriage to get you a mother.

What on earth made you think that a woman you barely knew would want a young child, or that she would instantly become a devoted mother to one she'd never met? What evidence did you have that made you believe that? Did you just think any woman would jump at the chance to be a mother if she could also be the wife of a good-looking professional musician? Was it your arrogance? Ignorance? Lust?

Summarizing that period of time in our lives, my father said:

> I had gotten married and I had hoped that my new
> wife would become your devoted mother which didn't
> work out that way at all, as you know. Anyway, I
> played the season in the pit band at the Albee for
> live shows. They had a different show in every
> week that ran seven days a week, early matinee and
> then evening.

By April or May of 1946, before I had turned three years old,
my father was living in San Diego, California where he had taken
a job playing in a band at a nightclub called Sherman's. I remained
with my grandparents, who were providing me with consistent and
loving care.

My father wrote the following about the night he met my
next stepmother:

> It was a Monday evening, my night off from work. I
> was playing with Jimmy James Orchestra at the time
> and Ruth Ann was working there. I had contemplated
> asking her for a date for some time and I had finally
> obtained the courage to ask. Behold, she accepted!
> After she finished work, I drove her home—to a
> beach house occupied by five other girls. We spent
> the evening talking and then went in swimming.
> The rest is history.

Ruth Ann, who was then twenty-five, and working at Sherman's
Nightclub as a cigarette girl, wrote,

> The first night I ever noticed Kenneth was May 27,
> 1946. Since he was off work, he proceeded to come
> in and bother me as I was doing mine. I finally made

a date with him for after work. We rode around first
and then went to my house. We talked lots, played
records and went swimming and much to my surprise
I had a wonderful time. We started going quite steady
and soon cared very much for each other.

According to Ruth Ann's written record of that time, she and my
father left San Diego in the fall, stopping to see her family in Kansas
and watching a World Series game in St. Louis "before we headed to
Nana & Granny's house."

We lived there with them until we came back to
Wichita and got married. You were still wetting the
bed at three years old—emotional stress. I had a room
across from yours and every night you dropped your
socks out of the crib. You didn't call me mommy, just
Ruthie, and I didn't push myself on you.

*Why would I call her mommy? Did my father introduce Ruth Ann to
me as my new mommy? Is that what I was told about Ginger? Did my
father or grandmother tell her that I was wetting the bed due to emotional
stress or did she come to that conclusion herself? I remember Nana talking
about me throwing my socks out of the crib and then crying or calling her
and she would come give them back to me. Did I fling my socks to the
floor to see if somebody would come, to prove to myself that I wasn't all
alone? Why was it so important to me to keep my socks in bed with me
at night? Is it possible that their smell comforted me somehow?*

Ruth describes the schedule in the expanded household during
those months:

I was working for Lever Brothers and went to
work every morning with Granny, who worked for
Westinghouse. We would leave at 7:00 or 7:30 in
the morning. Ken didn't get up until 9:30 or 10:00.

We'd all have supper together. Ken went to work 6 days a week, during the afternoon and all evening. He got home after midnight and sometimes I'd see him for just a few minutes or wait up for him but Monday was our night and we'd go out to dinner or to a movie or just someplace and talk.

Given that description, I wonder how much time I actually spent, during the months that followed, with either my father or with the tall, smiley, blond-haired woman destined to become my next mother. Sometime in the spring—I would guess around Mother's Day—Ruth Ann decided that she would take me to Kansas to meet her family.

In the blink of an eye, as they say, I found myself on a fast-moving passenger train with her, heading away from the stability, comfort and familiarity I had come to know in my grandparents' home. I assume my grandmother must have condoned this trip and probably spoken to me about what to expect on the train, assuring me I would have fun and that I would be okay. It was this trip, however, that gave rise to an incident that would both erode my self-image as well as impact my relationship with my soon-to-be new mother. The memory has remained consistent and vivid my entire life.

We spent one night on the moving train and the next night in a hotel in some city, Chicago perhaps. It was in that beige and white shaded hotel room that Ruth Ann decided—possibly because she'd overheard my grandmother beginning to teach me the alphabet—that I was surely old enough to recite my ABCs on demand; or, if not, she would tutor me in that performance.

I am tired. I miss Nana and Granny, and my daddy. I don't want to be in this strange room. I want to go to sleep . . . I can only say the first few letters. I can't make my brain work the way she wants. She is getting angry and I feel totally helpless. I want to hide. I am trying hard not to let my tears come but I can't stop them.

The longer I was unable to give Ruth Ann what she was demanding of me, the more agitated she became. Why she thought hitting me across my thighs with a Fuller Brush would elicit what she wanted, I cannot fathom, as both the unexpected action and the stinging pain only made me cry harder. After she used the brush in this way a few times, the monogrammed plate on the back suddenly came loose and fell to the floor. Maybe it startled her into recognizing what she was actually doing. At that point she abandoned her quest and nothing more was said about the ABCs.

I was trying so hard to please her when she got angry and hurt me and then I felt so lost and lonely and sad. Even though I eventually realized that she was desperately wanting to be seen as a good mother and wanting to impress her relatives by teaching me to "perform" in that way for them, and even though I ultimately forgave her, it took decades and the help of trained therapists to release that deeply buried hurt and sadness from my body and mind.

The next thing I knew, I was being arranged this way and that for what seemed like endless picture taking with my almost stepmother and various members of her family. Anxious, lonely and sad, I kept quiet, and kept smiling, doing my best to be a good little girl as I suspect my father told me to do. Talking nonstop, the woman who was to become his next wife read only the surface, never looking any deeper than my forced, superficial smiles, which, to her, confirmed just the opposite of everything I was feeling. I continued this charade throughout the onslaught of strangers exclaiming how pretty I was and what a sweet smile I had. I ate food I didn't like. I sat in unfamiliar chairs with my back straight, my dangling legs crossed at the ankles in an effort to emulate my grandmother's posture in social situations. I learned quickly what behavior pleased Ruth Ann. The more quickly I smiled, or did whatever she wanted, the more praise she received and the happier she was.

Nearly sixty years into the future, during one of her marathon long distance telephone calls, my mother's thoughts skipped backwards. As she started reminiscing about the past, I recorded her words:

> I wanted to bring you to Wichita partly to show you off, and partly to prove to myself that you would stay with me, and we came on the train and you never said anything about your Daddy in those four or five weeks and you seemed to be happy and then Ken called and said, 'Guess what? I can get a week off—how fast can you get ready for a wedding?' I about jumped through the phone and all that time you had never acted like you missed them. We tried to do nice things to entertain you. You didn't seem to miss them and I wanted to see what I could do with you . . .

I eventually came to understand that by that particular point in my young life, I had already begun unconsciously practicing what is now known as dissociation, a therapeutic term which Peter A. Levine, renowned developer of Somatic Experiencing therapy for trauma healing, describes as "a means of enabling a person to endure experiences that are at the moment beyond endurance." Any time I began to feel vulnerable, scared, or helpless, I would automatically try to make myself small and invisible so as not to be noticed. I would just energetically disappear and disconnect from my surroundings or from a situation that I had no control over. It is obvious to me now that this was a way of protecting myself when feelings of anxiety and fear arose. This coping mechanism followed me into adulthood. I can still feel that mechanism start to kick in when I feel unheard or misunderstood; I just want to disappear.

Not yet four years old, I was expected to perform as a flower girl at my father and Ruth Ann's wedding, which took place in a large church sanctuary lavishly decorated with flowers and candles. I have some vague recollection of a rehearsal that must have gone well.

When the actual moment arrived, however, with music playing and strangers watching, the aisle seemed overwhelmingly long.

My body freezes. I can't move. Ruth Ann becomes increasingly upset. She tries to push me forward. She hits me hard on my bottom but I still can't move. I am crying. Soon, completely exasperated, she turns her back on me and walks down the aisle towards my father.

Was I just left standing there alone? Was anyone else there? Was my crying audible? I assume my grandmother must surely have figured out what was going on and come to me and then taken me to sit with her.

In the posed wedding photographs from that long ago event, I'm standing next to one of the ring bearers whom I will become friends with years later. I'm clutching the decorative basket still filled with rose petals. I'm trying, and failing, to force my face into a smile. As I study the photograph years later, the most striking thing I notice is how much my face resembles my birth mother's features. I have

no recollection of anything in the hours or days that followed the wedding ceremony. My father and Ruth Ann enjoyed a "grand" honeymoon, described in great detail in her leather-bound vintage memory book, "Our Yesterdays," a wedding gift from her older sister. She recounts activities from movies to stage shows to radio shows to winning money on a last-minute bet at the horse races and "dancing the night away" at various famous night clubs in

Kansas City and Chicago. "In the meantime, Nana took Dawn back home so we could be alone."

Was I confused or anxious about what was going to happen next, traumatized in some way by the events around the wedding, or was I just relieved to be with my grandparents again in the familiar home I knew and felt safe in?

During another of my mother's long and loquacious telephone calls in the late 1990s, out of the blue she remarked, "I have prayed often for forgiveness . . . even at our wedding I whopped you on the bottom instead of talking to you sweetly and different times when you couldn't learn your ABCs and I probably was a child abuser and didn't know it . . . I didn't know beans about raising a child." I went into shock momentarily, realizing that she remembered that dreadful night in the hotel room. I felt a kind of relief that Mother had come to the awareness she voiced and that she had acknowledged those incidents. Before I could respond, however, she was already chattering on about something else entirely, and I let the moment pass without comment or closure. It was almost as if she forgot I was on the other end of the phone line and was just thinking out loud.

I wonder now when or how she became conscious of the fact that the way she had treated me was abusive? Why didn't she ever tell me she was sorry? Did she assume I wouldn't remember? Did she have any idea how much those incidents affected our relationship?

According to the copious notes Ruth Ann maintained during the first year of her marriage to my father, the three of us continued living with my grandparents for four more months until we moved into a furnished apartment of which I have no memory whatsoever. Six weeks after that we moved into a new "house with 5 rooms and a full basement." Ruth Ann writes how "swell it is to have a whole house to ourselves and to finally be able to send for and use the wedding gifts to entertain." Regarding Thanksgiving she writes that "Dawn was in Pittsburg (at the home of Nana's sister) with Nana and

Granny from Thursday till Sunday. We had a nice vacation and a big Thanksgiving dinner all alone. Lots of fun for four days!"

Studying a black and white photograph of "the brick house on Karen Avenue," which was surrounded by dirt and no landscaping whatsoever, I can access no memory of actually living there, no image of where I slept or what anything looked like inside that house. Though I possess no photographs of the interior of my grandparents' house either, I have distinctly vivid memories of parts of the large kitchen: an old treadle sewing machine in one corner that I loved watching my grandmother use; playing under a round wooden table on the black and white linoleum floor while she made pancakes, sometimes with blueberries in them; the adjoining dining room, and the drop leaf mahogany table with the pull out drawer lined with green felt to protect the silverware. I remember sitting next to my grandmother at that same table, enthralled as I watched her needlepoint new covers for the dining room chairs. I remember laying my head in her lap and her brushing my hair, an oft repeated, soothing act that made me feel so loved and cared for that I can never recall that sensation without feeling deep emotion and gratitude.

Another scene embedded in my memory is of kneeling with Nana by a twin bed, with a framed photograph of my father on the side table, in the same room as my crib (the bedroom my father grew up in, I now realize) putting my palms together the way Nana did and imitating her words: "Now I lay me down to sleep. I pray the Lord my soul to keep. If I should die before I wake pray the Lord my soul to take." This was followed by "God bless Daddy" and "God bless Nana and Granny," and so on. I didn't grasp the meaning of all the words at the time, of course, yet the intimacy of that repeated ritual created a safe space deep inside me which I later retreated to, repeating the words to myself when I was alone or lonely in my bed, or when I was missing my grandmother.

I have retained one notable memory from the short time I was in the new brick house with my father and Ruth Ann:

I am in the front seat of a car Ruth Ann is driving. I am holding onto a large metal

pot full of potatoes which someone has given us and that Ruth Ann set on my lap for me to hold. We are going down a steep hill when, without warning, the car door beside me swings open, the container on my lap tips over and I can see potatoes rolling down the hill. I am startled, afraid I am going to fall out of the car and roll down the hill too or crack my head open. Ruth Ann stops the car. She is angry. That means I have done something. wrong, but I don't know what . . . She retrieves the pan and a couple of potatoes. She slams my door shut, gets back in her side and finishes the drive, in complete silence. Later I hear Ruth Ann laughing while she is telling my father and the people who came to dinner about the potatoes rolling down the hill. She says nothing to me or about me, not even that she was relieved I didn't fall out of the car. She doesn't seem to even notice that I'm in the room. I feel forgotten, alone, and as if I am almost completely invisible.

There were no seat belts in those days but surely Ruth Ann shut the door on my side of the car. Wouldn't she have gotten me into the seat, then handed me the pot with the potatoes in it and shut the door before going around to her side of the car? Was I supposed to shut the door? How would I have the strength to do that with one arm when I was only three years old? Was she mostly perturbed about losing the potatoes she was going to cook for dinner and I just thought she was mad at me? Was she actually upset with herself for not making sure the door was shut and she projected the blame onto me? Did she even think at all about how I might have been feeling? I am now guessing that her laughter was likely a deflection from

at least some degree of guilt she must surely have felt after the unexpected
and unnerving event that occurred that day.

There was very little time to even begin to acclimate to the
new house or situation before everything changed again, as Ruth
Ann documented:

May 7, 1948: Ken lost his job at the Latin Quarter.

May 27, 1948: We sold all of our furniture during the
past 2 weeks & left Cincinnati for good today at 2:00
a.m. headed toward Memphis.

May 28, 1948: Ken left in a plane this morning to join
Ted Weems' band in Atlanta.

Years before reading Ruth Ann's notations, while I was
interviewing my father about his musical career, he said nothing
about losing his job, only that he had been working at the Latin
Quarter nightclub in Newport, Kentucky for about a year and was
doing well but that he was growing tired of working so late.

You'd start around 9 or 10 p.m. and work till 3 or
4 a.m. so you'd end up sleeping all morning. It was
while I was playing at the Latin Quarter that a friend
of mine came in one day and he was playing with
Ted Weems. He said he sure wished he could have
a steady job like mine. He was envious of my living
at home all the time and not traveling and he was
getting tired of the road so I said, 'Well, if you're
serious maybe we could trade. So he gave Ted Weems
notice and said he had a replacement. That's when I
went with Weems.

Is it possible my father just told Ruth Ann that he'd lost his job rather than
saying he wanted the change he described to me? Wouldn't being in a band

on the road be the same late hours with the additional stress of travel? Was he just growing bored with staying in one place? Was my existence a consideration at all? Is there any chance that my father thought he would go on the road and Ruth Ann would stay behind with me, or did he just assume they would take me with them, but then left the decision up to her because she was now "the mother"?

The first entry from the Children's Home file reads:

> **SUMMARY RECORD 6-4-48:** Stepmother, Mrs. Kenneth C. Armor came to the Home to make arrangements for placing Dawn as she wanted to travel with Mr. Armor, who plays with Ted Weems Band and said that they couldn't take Dawn with them.

Five

The "Home"

*. . . adverse experiences early in life can impair brain architecture,
with negative effects lasting into adulthood.*
~ Harvard University Center on the Developing Child

*Our brains are shaped by our early experience . . . being validated by
being heard and seen is a precondition for feeling safe.*
~ Bessel Van Der Kolk

The first typewritten notes in the Children's Home SUMMARY
RECORD continue as follows:

> After much consideration and deliberation, the
> mother's conscience seemed to bother her over leaving
> the child, finally decided that the Home was the place
> for her for about one year.

I have no recollection at all
regarding the actual move into
the Wichita Children's Home,
though it must surely have been
unsettling and confusing. I must
have felt powerless as I was forced
to adjust to yet another change,
and to being left in that huge
imposing brick building with no
familiar spaces or faces.

The third note in my record from the Home which
is undated, states, Dawn is quite a sweet child—does

not seem to have a sense of security; however, she is not difficult to manage. She gets much pleasure playing with her dolls. She has brown eyes and long hair. Will go to kindergarten this fall.

I find the words "does not seem to have a sense of security" both laughable and depressing. I remember well that my three dolls were my only familiar companions in that brand new communal environment. I pretended they were my children, talking to them, kissing them good night and tucking them all in together under a little blanket on the small wooden bed that my new stepmother's older sister and her husband had provided for me. I often "read" to them from the ten by twelve inch hard-boarded, illustrated copy of *The Brimful Book,* given to me the previous year by Nana's older sister. I guarded that treasured gift, which has now been shared with children and grandchildren, the way other young children clutched their teddy bears. The words, even before I could read them, and the pictures on each page of that book provided me with solace, decreased my sense of isolation, and somehow helped me feel less alone.

I'm uncertain how many very young children were already living in the wing of the building I was placed in. I feel sure I was one of the youngest in the group, although the others were, at most, only a year or two older. A row of simple steel, military style twin beds, maybe ten or twelve in number, were lined up along each side of the long rectangular room where we slept. There was a door at the far end of the room that opened to a fire escape. Not all the beds were filled. The bathroom, and a linoleum-floored, rectangular play room were near the entrance to this dormitory-like space on one side; the rooms occupied by the woman who was in charge of us were on the other side. The image in my head of that person, whose name was Mrs. Hamilton, is of a tall, sharp-edged, boney old woman of harsh demeanor, with graying hair wrapped into a tight bun on the back of her head. She wore false teeth which she kept in a glass by her bed at night. This unusual sight was reported by every little girl who was invited into that space, usually as a reward for some kind of "good behavior" and, finally one evening I actually viewed it myself. Whenever one of us cried in response to a rebuke from Mrs. Hamilton—she would shake her finger at the offender, and raise her voice, saying, "Stop that crying or I'm going to put you out on the fire escape and you'll freeze that way." The threat was always ominous though I can imagine it worked more quickly as a deterrent during the snowy, midwestern winters. On Saturday mornings we all had designated work time after breakfast and before our play time because, as our caretaker repeatedly reminded us, "Every little girl has to do her work." Each of us was assigned a task, which remained the same every week. Mine was in the bathroom, cleaning the toilets. Another child scrubbed the sinks while I was on my knees in one stall at a time "making the toilets shine" inside and out, and then scrubbing the surrounding black and white diamond shaped floor tiles. I remember no other work assignment in the nearly two years I lived in the Children's Home.

Was any thought put into which child did which job? How were those assignments made? Did we have any choice in the matter? Who did my job on the occasional weekends when I was taken out to visit Ruth Ann's parents? I presume the work assignments were meant as training for future housewives. Did a maintenance staff clean more thoroughly when we were elsewhere?

My father was on the road with the band that summer playing mostly "one nighters" and writing lengthy, amorous, letters to my stepmother, who had apparently taken a temporary part-time job in Wichita prior to actually joining my father on the road, in order to help them out financially. I suppose I must surely have spent some time with her, either in her parents' home or maybe in one of her sisters' homes while Ruth Ann was still in Wichita, and yet I have no specific memories of that occurring.

In a letter postmarked June 1, 1948, from Atlanta, Georgia, my father lists the band's itinerary for the next six weeks. He follows that with a detailed account of money he is sending to his wife, as well as money he has spent before writing the following:

I'm amazed at the folks' attitude about putting Dawn in a home. Gee honey these are times that get me down. I had just seen the picture *The Mating of Millie* (A romantic comedy about a child in an orphanage hoping to be adopted.) when I read your letter about what to do with Dawn and I felt pretty bad about it. I am being constantly torn between two principles on the matter, but I guess it will all work out.

I will never know exactly what two principles my father was debating but I am astonished by the naivete in his statement, and by his choice to deny or ignore both his feelings and his responsibilities. From my current vantage point, I can well imagine how upset my grandparents must have been when they were told I was going to be "put into a home," given their intimate experience with the instability of my first few years of life, but I am astonished by the naivete in his statement, and by his choice to deny or ignore both his feelings and his responsibilities. From my current vantage point, I can well imagine how upset my grandparents must have been when they were told I was going to be "put into a home," given their intimate experience with the instability of my first few years of life, and their great effort to allay its adverse effects by taking me in and providing me with physical and emotional refuge. Their offering of security, consistency, caring touch, and unconditional love during my second year of life may have quite literally saved my life.

I remember my grandmother responding to something I asked her years later. Since I had no memory of the actual transition of leaving their home, I thought it must surely have been difficult and upsetting for me. However, Nana had replied, "Oh, no, you were excited and happy to be with your daddy." She then added, "Your grandad and I felt that it was time for your father to begin to take responsibility for you" and something about feeling that if he didn't take that responsibility then, they were afraid he might never do so.

Had they assumed that my father and my newest stepmother would take me with them on the road when my dad made that decision, hoping perhaps he would find a way to settle down by the time I needed to enter school since kindergarten was not mandatory? Is it possible that hearing about me being taken to the Children's Home contributed to my grandfather's nervous breakdown which I only recently learned he suffered around that time?

About ten letters later, my father mentions me again, saying:

> I'm glad your mother and sister went out with you to the Boarding Home. Their being more satisfied makes me feel better too. Have you said much to Dawn about it? If so, is there any bad reaction? Honestly honey, I think I would just junk this job if I thought Dawn was going to be the least bit unhappy in that home.

What was I told about this move? Did Ruth Ann paint a picture of a happy place with lots of children for me to play with and nice people who would take good care of me? Did she promise I would see her every weekend? Did she truly believe I would be better off living with strangers in another new and different place while she was still living with her parents in the same city? Did I ever consciously think about or wonder if I was ever going to have a real mother, or if I was even ever going to see my father again? She had obviously made the decision to leave me in the Home so even if I'd had a negative reaction to whatever I was told, she wouldn't have told my father.

In the same piece of correspondence, my father tells Ruth Ann that he would like it very much if she would plan to be with me on my birthday.

In my mind I've been thinking about us getting together at the latest in Memphis when we open there the July 16 but it only seems fair, or rather, it would seem a pity for neither of us to be there for Dawn's birthday when it would only mean a wait of a week or five days.

My father ends another letter by going and give her a big hug and kiss for me.

I wasn't quite five years old. I have no memory of Ruth Ann telling me what my father is suggesting or ever hugging and kissing me and saying it was from my Daddy. How would it have made any sense to me, or made me feel any better, to tell me the names of all the different cities and states my daddy was going to? Could that be part of the reason my grandfather bought me a colorful wooden puzzle of all the states and helped me until I could almost put it together by myself? Once I was able to do that, he set up a game of timing me again and again for fun, something I now recognize as a brilliant teaching strategy on his part.

In a missive to Ruthie darling from Boston, Massachusetts. postmarked June 19, 1948, my father tells his wife how happy he was to receive her Father's Day card and one from me also. "Please thank Dawn for me & tell her Daddy will write her a letter as soon as he gets a chance."

Did Ruth Ann pick out a card for me to send to Daddy for Father's Day? Try to help me sign my name or sign it for me? Or, as I suspect, did she simply buy a card and pretend it was from me because she thought it would be cute? Did my father ever write me a letter? Was I told he was going to? If so, did I wait and hope for one that never came?

A couple of weeks later my father refers to me once again, asking his dearest wife to "Give my love & kisses to Dawn—and don't forget about her honey."

What made me burst into tears reading the words 'don't forget about her honey'? Why did my father write those words? Maybe she hadn't said anything about me in her letters in a while? Was it possible his conscience was bothering him?

In his letter a few days later, my father mentions my birthday again.

> You didn't say anything about staying in Wichita till after Dawn's birthday. How do you feel about that? In my mind I am planning for you to come & join me in Memphis right after her birthday. Is that OK with you?

My father writes to his wife about what it's like for him to be playing lead with a good band. He includes all sorts of details regarding how they get back and forth from their jobs, and what he does in his off time. He says he wishes they could find a way to add some pin money while traveling, before adding, "But I think we will make out okay and we'll have a lot of fun."

The note on the back side of a slightly blurry photo taken on my birthday seems to indicate that perhaps Ruth Ann helped arrange for the party even though she wasn't actually there since she had joined my father six days earlier. I don't recognize any of the children in the picture and, unlike my party the previous year, I haven't even a snippet of recall regarding that event.

After decades, I still have several clear sensory and visual memories from living in the Children's Home. Something happened in the playroom one day when we were left unsupervised for a brief time. Two girls got into some sort of tussle over a doll or a toy and the upset escalated, leading to the following scene later that night.

We children have nothing on except our bleached white panties. We are all being made to walk in a circle in front of the

wall of the dark wooden cubbies that hold our clean underwear and pajamas. Mrs. Hamilton is pacing back and forth and waving the large red wooden paddle, which usually hangs on a hook on the side of the cubbies. She is demanding one of us tell her what happened but nobody speaks.

Were we all waiting for someone else to say something, too stressed by the imminent threat of bodily harm to speak, or were we rendered mute by some secret, telepathic choice to remain silent and not tattle?

Mrs. Hamilton is making us walk faster and faster until we are all almost prancing like little ponies and before long, we are all crying.

I can't be certain if the paddle was actually used on any one of us that night or if it was simply brandished as an imminent possibility, nor do I remember who or what brought closure to this incident, or how we all made it into our beds.

SUMMARY RECORD 9-7-48: Dawn entered kindergarten today. She has developed very much since her arrival here. Is becoming quite plump and is growing noticeably responsive . . .

My memories of anything to do with my first formal school experiences are minimal, though one in particular has remained very clear and virtually the same each time I've recalled it. It has to do with my first day in a school classroom setting, and a little boy named Gary whose hair was as white as clean snow. He began crying inconsolably as soon as his mother left. His despair may have eclipsed my own anxiety and uneasiness, or perhaps I perceived a kindred spirit. What I remember most clearly is that I felt compelled to comfort him. The smiling, dark-haired teacher, who had tried briefly to distract this distraught little boy, needed to put her attention on the other parents dropping off their young children. My mission was obvious. I stuck to Gary like glue the rest of the day. He eventually stopped crying though I don't think he ever smiled.

When the time came to roll out our rugs on the polished hardwood floor for quiet time, he and I lay down next to each other. Neither of us went to sleep as some of the other children seemed to. I kept my attention on Gary the entire time. At the end of the nap time, each child was given a small carton of milk and two graham crackers. I had never liked those hard, dry crackers, which I'd encountered before at the Children's Home and offered mine to Gary. His refusal seemed to increase some unspoken, fragile bond that helped us both survive the first day of being thrown together with strangers in a strange land called kindergarten.

I have recently read studies suggesting that trauma experienced during childhood can increase a person's ability to intuitively understand another person's mental and emotional states, and that this influence is long-standing. Pain can be a doorway to greater compassion for others. I now recognize that my sensitivity to loneliness and sadness in others first began to manifest itself in my encounter with a white-haired, never-to-be-forgotten little boy, on a sunny September day when I was five years old.

Near the end of that September, during a series of one nighters with the band, Ruth Ann was driving while my dad slept after a job. At around 2 a.m., she stopped at a service station to use the bathroom. As she was walking from the restroom back to the car, a drunk driver in a truck came speeding through and hit her. She was thrown up onto the windshield of the truck, shattering the glass, and then fell back onto the ground as the driver sped away. My sleeping father was awakened by the sound. He and a couple of men who had witnessed this shocking event managed to get Ruth Ann into the car and to the nearest hospital in the very small town of Rhome, Texas, where she was given transfusions, stitches for the deep gash over her eye, and a few x-rays.

It is unclear the exact number of days Ruth Ann spent in that hospital before my dad was able to get her into a compartment on a train and transferred to a much larger hospital in Wichita where her parents and two sisters lived. The more extensive x-rays taken in that hospital showed compound skull and sinus fractures. The doctor Ruth Ann later credited with "saving my life" told her it was a miracle that she had lived through her injuries, that she would have to lie quietly on her back for one to two months to heal, and that she could still die.

> **10-6-48 SUMMARY RECORD:** Mr. Armor came to see Dawn today to take her to Wesley Hospital to visit Mrs. Armor who met quite a serious accident when she and Mr. Armor were in Texas. She was brought to Wichita as soon as she was able to travel.

I still retain a vague impression of being taken into the hospital room and either standing or perhaps sitting on Daddy's lap by Ruth Ann's bedside. One of her eyes was swollen shut and her long hair was all matted. I remember her saying that they couldn't comb her hair because she had too many cuts on her head. I think the visit was brief, probably so as not to tire her. I have no idea how much time, if any, I may have spent with my father before it was time to say goodbye to him again when he took me back to the Home that day.

I experience an aching sadness thinking about what it might have been like for me to see Daddy for what must have been such a short time. I find myself wondering how it was for him as well as what I might have been feeling when he brought me back to the home. Or is it possible that someone else took me back? Did I cry when Daddy and I said goodbye or did I simply bury whatever emotions I might have been feeling? I have no memory of that parting.

The dozens of letters I found when cleaning out the massively overcrowded house of a long-time hoarder after Ruth Ann's death reveal that my father sent tenderly affectionate and encouraging letters to her daily. Eventually, she was allowed to sit up in her hospital bed for five minutes at a time and write letters to him.

Her handwriting in the first few letters he received is uneven and childlike. One letter begins with her apologizing for her selfishness and promising she will do better. In another, she seems to be going through some sort of mental crisis.

> Darling, I want another chance to prove to you that I can be a good wife. I'm afraid I'd grown into a griping nagging person. My conscience seems to bother me so. When I am well, you and Dawn and I will be together again. I do love her. I am sorry that I said such awful things about her.

Did this uncharacteristic expression come from a medicated state? What awful things had she said about me and when did she say them? Was this another reason she made the decision to take me to live in the Children's Home? Did she think they would somehow shape me into being a "good little girl" or one that she'd be better able to manage or was she just putting off having to actually take on the responsibilities of motherhood?

By the end of October, her letters reveal that Ruth Ann was able to get out of bed and take a few steps before being released to her parents' home to continue her bed rest, recovery and rehabilitation. In a letter written after I was brought to see her, she writes about me giving them all a synopsis of a play that the children from the Home were taken to see and how detailed it was. She then reiterates that she loves me now, saying she felt it was a duty or obligation before, but that now she actually feels she loves me.

What changed her mind? She had spent very little time with me. Did she just want to reassure my Dad or think that was what he needed or wanted to hear? Could her mother have said something to her about it?

In a letter dated November 4, 1948 my father reassures Ruth Ann that he has everything planned out and asks her again not to worry about her condition, and to have faith in her doctor. Towards the end of the letter, he again assures her that no matter what happens he loves her, saying that is "something in me to stay."

> It wouldn't make any difference if you came back to me with one eye, a wooden leg and flat feet. Now don't cry sweetheart, just be happy and have nice thoughts . . .

In another of his daily letters, my father urges his wife, yet again, to please take good care of herself.

> Please don't do anything that will retard your recuperation baby. Make sure to eat lots and just think about the future. And remember that everything will work itself out okay.

As she begins writing longer letters to my father, Ruth Ann's cognitive abilities seem to improve, and her persistently directive personality reasserts itself. Even though my father pleads with her, again and again, to let him take care of things and to just concentrate on getting her strength back, she begins giving him explicit suggestions on everything from how to deal with the bills and the insurance company to how to make some extra money selling the Christmas cards they had apparently already purchased and planned to resell for a profit. His letters, meanwhile, recount how busy he is rehearsing, working, getting their car in shape and fixing up their trailer in preparation for her return.

A couple of weeks later Ruth Ann is still harping on the card selling, pointing out various ways for my father to sell them door to door. She returns to the theme at the end of still another letter, mentioning to her husband that he is so handsome, no one will be able to refuse buying cards from him. He continues to give her updates on his daily activities, including everything he does on his days off and how much money he is spending on specific items, and urging her not to try to do too much too soon. At that time, the band had been playing for an extended period of time at the Aragon Ballroom on Lick Pier in Santa Monica and my father broaches the possibility of Ruth Ann bringing me with her when she is able to rejoin him. She responds by saying:

> **For the first time, I can truthfully say that I want to but don't believe it would be best. She is well adjusted here and seems satisfied . . . I really think some of this has been good for her. She seems much better behaved than when I had her. It will be different when I have her again, honey I'll have better luck now, because I now love her and I want to have her. Before I didn't want her, I just thought I had to do it, but my heart wasn't into it . . . I can see how wrong I was. But I don't see how I could manage. There would be so much noise and work to do, extra washing, etc. When I come to you, I shan't be really well. So, don't have your hopes too high. I do want her though . . . but sickness and a child in such a small trailer. Do you think I should?**

It is hard to believe her words. Was there any truth at all to what she was saying to my father in this letter? How and when did she come to the decision that she actually loved me? It seems pretty clear that what she truly wants is to be alone with my father, that she doesn't really want me around or to have to feel responsible for me. Did Daddy really believe what she was telling him or did he simply abdicate to her in the matter?

Throughout her lifetime, Ruth Ann had a way of saying things that made it clear she wasn't really asking a question; she was, rather, pointing out the other person's flawed logic. If someone disagreed with her, or presented a different point of view, she would just keep talking and saying the same thing over and over again, perhaps in some slightly different way until the person who couldn't get a word in edgewise simply gave in to whatever she was wanting.

Was she even consciously aware of her obsessive chatter or of the effect it had on the people who she was talking to? Did anyone ever try to point it out to her? Where did she learn that? No one else in her family even came close to such a habit. Ruth Ann didn't seem capable of silence or reflection. I can't recall her ever asking someone else their opinion about anything. Is it possible that her compulsive talking was to cover up some anxiety or insecurity she was feeling inside?

My father continued to write detailed and romantic letters to Ruth Ann while her letters become more and more specifically directive, particularly in regard to their finances. "Are you writing all your expenses down? Please do." In one of his letters, my father pleads again with his wife not to worry about things or do anything that might slow down her recuperation. He asks her once again to let him handle the hospital bills.

> A husband is responsible for his wife's bills, and if I don't want to pay them what they say it's up to them to contact me, not you. If they want to know anything you tell them to just take it up with me.

She writes back telling him she can't forget the hospital bills and basically disagreeing with the way he wants to handle things. It becomes obvious that telling her not to worry or not to think about money is like telling a zebra it doesn't have stripes. She goes ahead and argues with the hospital about the bill and she contacts the insurance company.

My father proposes to sell their Mercury. She objects. He proposes they sell the trailer, laying out why it would ultimately save them money. Ruth Ann counters with what she thinks would be best. My father gets a speeding ticket and a $50 fine. He apologizes, asking his wife to please not be "too disgusted with me" and saying he really wasn't exceeding the limit that much.

Ruth Ann lost her long, blond hair after the accident and was unable to bleach what she had left. She writes my father describing various styles for her short, dark hair, making jokes about how she may look now. It seems fairly obvious that she is using humor as a cover for her worry about appearing less attractive to my father and to other people. My father writes back that her hair style is not what is important to him and to just concentrate on getting her strength back.

By mid-December, Ruth Ann seems to be thinking about clothing she feels she will be needing. She writes telling my father it will cost less to buy some things before coming to California and asking if he can send her some money. She tells him how many Christmas cards she has sold and urges him, yet again, to please try to sell some of the cards. She reminds him to keep them in his car so they are handy, ending with, "Let me know if you have tried."

When my father sends a clipping about a specific kind of doll that he thinks I might like as a Christmas present, Ruth Ann writes back describing the several dolls I already have before saying, "Do you think we should give her another doll? Don't you believe she would enjoy other things more? Next year maybe she will need a new dolly—do you agree?"

Clearly Daddy backed down at that point and deferred to her on the matter. Was it because he really thought she was right, because he didn't want to belabor the issue, or simply because he lacked the will or the energy to pursue a different point of view?

These lengthy pieces of correspondence between Ruth Ann and my father point to specific and repeated patterns, especially in relationship to money, that will contribute to the disintegration of their relationship less than a decade later.

As the holidays approach, my father asks his wife,

> How do they handle the Christmas situation where
> Dawn is? I do hope Santa remains Santa. Dawn should
> keep thinking that for a couple years yet . . . Honey
> do you tell Dawn that we're all going to be together
> soon? Honest honey, I don't want to put that off for
> too long regardless.

Ruth Ann responds to some of my father's questions while ignoring others and seems to be doing her best to convince my father of the perfectly wonderful time I will have during the Christmas holidays.

> I spoke with the supervisor and they are getting candy,
> gifts and everything . . . they will be having a party
> almost every night out there next week. Yes, Dawn
> still believes in Santa. Either Fern or Mama will have
> her on Christmas day. This will be a Christmas for
> her to remember!

Did she say all that to my father because she assumed all kids at that age cared about at Christmas time is how many presents they receive? Did I understand that she was leaving to go be with my daddy and yet I didn't get to go? Did I have any feelings about that or had I just given up hoping or wishing for such things?

In her next letter, Ruth Ann expresses great disappointment that my father has been unable to get leave from the band to fly back to Wichita for Christmas and to accompany her on the return trip. She laments the fact that he won't get to meet her sister's new baby before telling my father that he should have approached the matter in a different way. Weems had apparently not taken my father's request well, and recommended that he hire a nurse to be with his wife on the train.

Daddy responds to her comment with a hint of irritation, as well as relief that he needn't be concerned about my having a good Christmas without him or his wife.

> Yes, it is too bad I won't see Doris's baby, but after all
> I won't even get to see Dawn . . . I'm so glad to hear
> you say that her Christmas will be a nice one.

When my father urges his wife, yet again, to fly to California, she writes that she will be arriving at the LA train station the morning of December 23. "To tell the truth I'm scared to death to ride a plane now. I guess the accident did that to me, so I'll come by train." My dad's reply included a comment about how odd it was that her accident made her afraid to fly since there was no plane involved before assuring her that he will take his alarm clock and sleep overnight at the depot, to make sure he is there in plenty of time to greet her.

Other than going to a circus performance for the first time in my life, and being completely mesmerized by the trapeze artists and tight rope walkers, I can access no memories at all regarding that Christmas season, either at the Children's Home, or anywhere else.

∞

I'm unsure at what point during my stay in "The Home" the following incident took place. The scene, however, has remained indelibly etched in my mind.

> **The tall skinny girl with the straight light-blond hair is tied to her bed with strips of sheets. She is on her back. Her arms are stretched above her head, each one tied at the wrist to one side of the bars that form the bed's head frame. Her legs are separated so that one ankle is tied to each side of the bottom of the bed frame. I feel so bad for her. I feel scared. She isn't crying or moving.**

What did she do wrong? Why is she being punished like that? I feel sad. I look away and try to pretend I don't really see her.

Is there any chance that being tied to her bed was an intervention meant to cure sleep walking? Or maybe she tried to sneak out of the building in the middle of the night? I think she was in the Home, or at least in the section I was in, for only a brief period. Every time that memory comes up and the scene replays itself in my mind, I wonder where she might have been sent and why.

Another lucid memory from my time living in the Children's Home that has stayed with me began as a punishment, for what I have no idea, yet it turned out to be a significant and comforting experience.

I am in the very last bed at the end of the room past several empty beds, right next to the fire escape. This isolation is how Mrs. Hamilton punishes any of us who have done something she deems unacceptable and I'm having trouble getting to sleep in the bed without my dolls next to me, but I don't feel afraid, just a little more alone than usual. I'm looking out of the high window when I hear a voice coming out of the moon as a cloud passes over it. I decide it must be God. The voice seems comforting somehow. I feel less alone. It feels as if I now have a secret protector.

Although the exact words I heard that night disappeared long ago, I've never forgotten the essence of the event. In hindsight, I am aware that this was my first spiritual—or what some would call mystical—experience, in terms of making a connection to something outside myself and feeling I was not all alone.

According to the Children's Home medical records, I had the chicken pox in January of 1949. The most momentous visual and sense memory I have retained during the time I was living in the Children's Home occurred in that month. Ruth Ann was apparently in Wichita to have some dental work done related to her accident and head injuries and came to see me.

I'm wearing my warm, yellow, footed pajamas, alone in the second-floor dormitory room with only my dolls, eating lunch. During the chicken pox outbreak, I was the last one to have a pox detected during the daily inspections. An older girl comes in with a tray of food for me. She tells me I am going to have a visitor soon and leaves. I don't feel hungry. I don't know who is coming to see me . . . Ruth Ann walks into the room and sits down on the bed next to mine. She is wearing a full-length coat with a fur collar. Smiling at first, she starts talking right away. I can't think of what to say. She's talking so fast I don't have time to think. I wish my daddy was here instead of her. She doesn't touch me at all. Her smile fades and she is looking at me as if I've done something wrong. She's upset. I am trying not to cry just as she says, "Well, if you aren't going to talk to me, I might as well leave." I can't think fast enough of something to say. As she walks out of the room, my tears spill out. I get out of my bed and hurry toward the doors leading out to the hallway. I make my way down the wide polished wooden stairs, all by myself, as fast as I can. When I reach the bottom, I hear voices from the dining room but there is no one in the hallway. I

arrive at the tall, double doors with glass in the top half. I try to open one of the doors but it doesn't budge. On my tiptoes, I can see her walking toward the taxi cab at the end of the long sidewalk. I want her to turn around and see me. I open my mouth to call, 'please don't leave. I'm sorry, please come back,' but no sound comes out. She gets in the cab. It pulls away from the curb and disappears. I slowly walk back through the hallway and climb the stairs. I crawl back into my bed and curl up inside myself.

The taxi was clearly waiting curbside, and Ruth Ann didn't even take off her coat. She couldn't have been planning to stay much longer than a few minutes with me that day in any case! Did she just come so she could tell my father that she had seen me? What did she tell him about that visit?

That scene has replayed itself in my mind any number of times across the years. While writing about it, my entire body began convulsing with hot angry sobs that seemed endless. I found myself on my feet kicking and punching the air with my fists, my breath spewing out in howls and growls. It wasn't so much rage that erupted in me but an experience of power unleashed. My energy filled the room around me and the space outside my window.

> **May 17, 1949. DISMISSED** to her father and mother. They thought she could go with them in their trailer and have a wonderful summer.

Studying an old black and white photograph of my father standing in front of the mini mobile home he often referred to as the "blather" for reasons I've yet to figure out, it seems

barely big enough for two people, let alone a third. I have no idea where I slept inside the trailer or any image whatsoever of the inside.

I do retain a collage of impressions from life in the trailer park: the ice man who drove into the open space in the middle of the area once a week or so, opened the door of his truck, and picked up huge blocks of ice with a big tong-like utensil to carry them to various recipients; my dad's tall and cheerful whistling friend, who I would eventually figure out was Elmo Tanner, the well-known Whistling Troubadour and singer featured on a number of records with the Ted Weems Orchestra. He helped my dad improve his whistling skills, which I was always fascinated by in later years though I could never get past a couple of notes myself. Mr. Tanner had a son near my age, called Little Elmo, whom I often played with.

The most memorable incident from that summer occurred when my father took me to the ocean—actually Galveston Bay along the Gulf of Mexico. When I was reluctant to walk into the water, he put me on his shoulders. The sea water was nearly up to his chest when he tripped on something and we both went down. Although it was surely only a matter of a few seconds before my father pulled me up and out of the water, flailing and coughing, the shock, compounded a couple of summers later by another water related trauma, had repercussions for years to come.

RE-ENTERED 9-6-49: Mrs. Armor returned Dawn to the Home for the school year . . . she had a grand time going with her parents in the trailer.

Did the person making these notes actually talk with me about my summer, or did Ruth Ann simply wax eloquent about what a great time I had? Did I really readjust instantly to the change back to living in the Children's Home? I have no memory at all of the transition.

In a two-column article in the Women's Activities Section of the San Francisco Chronicle for Sunday, October 30, 1949, the headline reads: "**The Band Plays On . . .** and the Orchestra Wives Keep Electric Plates Burning." There are two large photos. One of the photos is of three women and two children, both four years old. The second photo, captioned "Gin rummy while the band rehearses" shows Ruth Ann sitting in the foreground at a table with another woman. The article states that "The Armors had a red brick house in Cincinnati; sold it and their furniture for a chance to travel." It mentions that "the wife of Elmo Tanner, the whistler, was not present that day as she was picking up Little Elmo, age six, from school." A bit further down in the article, this line appears: "Mrs. Armor's daughter, Dawn, was an orchestra child, too, until she had to enter school this fall. She lives with her maternal grandmother in Wichita."

I can visualize Ruth Ann in the interview for the newspaper article chiming in with the misinformation. Perhaps her conscience was still bothering her in regard to leaving me behind and placing me in a residential institution? Maybe she couldn't admit, even to herself, that she wanted more time alone with my father without having to take care of a young child she barely knew. Maybe she had spoken to her parents about taking care of me and they either agreed and then changed their minds or weren't able to and she just went on pretending that I wasn't living in a children's home?

Grandma's husband was usually settled in a tall backed over-stuffed chair whose seat was dented from his weight and saturated with his smell even when he wasn't there. I remember him as always having an open newspaper in front of his face which he would put down only to walk the short distance to the dinner table when his wife called "Soup's on," even though there was hardly ever any soup on the table. After a quick head bob and muttered prayer which was so short that I barely had time to close my eyes, my new Grandpa kept his face bent over his dinner scarfing down everything on the plate as if he hadn't eaten in days. He'd then sop up any bits of food along with the sauce or gravy still on the plate with a small piece of bread, put the bread in his mouth, drain his cup of whatever liquid he was drinking, push his chair back, and go into the bedroom without a word before I was half done eating. My new grandma, however, always seemed to study her food before taking a bite. She would continue her contemplation as she began chewing, slowly and silently, as if she might be taking mental notes. When I stayed in their house overnight, I slept between the folds of a sheet and blanket spread over the dark green overstuffed couch in the living room. Grandma would make breakfast for the two of us the next morning, her husband having left hours earlier to begin delivering laundry, a job he'd had for years, as far as I know. On the mornings there had been a milk delivery, Grandma seemed to take great delight in letting me pour the rich cream that floated at the top of the glass milk bottles on the bowl of oatmeal she always made for me.

A short article that appeared in Ruth Ann's hometown newspaper later states that "Ruth Ann and her husband Ken Armor are having a grand time touring the country in their luxury trailer with the Ted Weems Orchestra." Yet another newspaper entry that appeared in the *Wichita Eagle* says that my father and his wife, "the former Ruth Ann Rogers of this city," visited her parents and the family of her sister. This information is followed by the statement that "Kenneth and Ruth Ann are on tour year-round and enjoy life immensely. They live in a deluxe trailer house and are at home immediately wherever they are. The Weems band just finished engagements in Galveston and Oklahoma City and goes next to the Lakes in Wisconsin."

Why did Ruth Ann feel such a need to embellish the truth? Was she exaggerating to make herself look better or to impress her friends and family? Did she feel embarrassed in some way because her husband wasn't making more money or that his salary wasn't enough to enable them to actually have a larger and more luxurious mobile home? And did she just try not to think about me at all?

I have few recollections from my first-grade school year beyond a long-lingering and pleasurable sense memory of learning to print letters. I loved practicing this new skill on the special paper we were given for that purpose with a top and bottom base line and a broken line in the middle. By the end of the year, along with the delight of starting to sight read *Dick and Jane* books, we were learning how to write in cursive, which I found even more exhilarating. The records I requested and received from the Children's Home some sixty years after I lived there included the report card from that first year in an elementary school which was named after the woman who wrote one of my favorite books—read under my bedcovers with a flashlight far into the night some years later—Louisa May Alcott. On the last page of the report, in the space reserved for the quarterly notes, my first-grade teacher writes that I am above my grade level in reading and writing, before stating, "Dawn needs to get books from the City Library and read aloud this summer to keep up speed and increase eye span." City libraries were not in my foreseeable future. However, my paternal grandmother's interest in reading books to me when I lived with her and my grandfather, and their habit of continuing to gift me with books, helped cultivate my passion for reading, which from a very early age became a refuge for me, a place I could disappear into. I began writing a novel entitled *Going to Mars* at around age nine, keeping the pages under my mattress. I showed it to one person only, Nana, when she and my grandfather were visiting our home. After reading the entire ten or twelve pages handwritten on lined notebook paper, she said to me, "You will be a writer and you will publish a book someday."

The last entry in my Children's Home records reads:

5-26-50 DISMISSED: Dawn is going
with her parents traveling over the country.

I actually spent the better part of that summer, including my seventh birthday, in the security and warm embrace of my grandparents in Charlotte, North Carolina, where they were living for a short time. Nana did not continually cuddle or coddle me, yet I always felt unconditionally embraced and loved by her. She paid attention to me. She listened to me. I knew I could trust her. I could be myself.

My father left Ted Weems sometime in August of 1950, the month after I had turned seven. Forty years later I asked him what prompted his decision to quit at that particular time.

> Well, each month I sort of got a little more worn out from being on the road all the time plus I felt it was a young man's business and not conducive to having a family . . . I had a need to settle down gnawing at me you could say. I had a little girl and you weren't supposed to go traveling around with a baby girl.

Section Two

Life Shaping Psychological Effects

Six

A Few (Nearly) Normal Years

A single image can split open the hard seed of the past and soon
memories pour forth from every direction.
~ Mary Kerr

We ache all our lives to be loved unconditionally,
to be seen as we truly are without judgement . . .
~ Jan Frazier

When my father left his job with the Ted Weems Orchestra, he and I and my stepmother, Ruth Ann, stayed with her parents for a short time. The day before I was to begin second grade, my father drove me through the route I was supposed to walk to get to the school I'd be attending. The next morning, I was nervous and worried that I wouldn't remember the way, yet I felt powerless and I seemed to have no choice but to start walking. I didn't notice any other kids. A few blocks into the walk, my heart began to pound when a large, long-haired dog seemed to appear out of nowhere and began moving in my direction. Having had little to no experience with any canines at that point in my life, I had no idea what to do.

The closer the dog came, the more anxious I felt. I was frozen in my tracks when, to my immense relief, my father appeared. He had been slowly following me in his car to make certain I got to the school okay. He showed me how to hold the back of my hand out for the dog to sniff. I could see that he wasn't the least bit nervous as he then began petting the dog. I worked up my courage enough to follow his example and have used it the rest of my life. He then smiled at me, told me to get into the car, and drove me to the school.

I still remember how protected and relieved it made me feel to know that my father had been watching me, and how grateful I was to see him. On that day my father became the man my grandmother had always told me he was, when she assured me that I would be with him someday. He became my hero. I felt claimed by him at last.

I recall nothing about that particular school building or classroom, which I believe I only attended for a couple of weeks. Since I don't remember ever walking all the way to the school, I am guessing that my father decided to drive me there each day and then stopped somewhere to have coffee and a little time to himself. I imagine he was also scouring the want ads in the local newspaper, searching for any job he might be able to secure having more or less left his musical career behind.

We soon moved into a housing development known as Hilltop Manor, which was built originally by the federal government during the war to house defense workers and their families. After the war ended, the units were sold to a Residential Housing Association, and another four hundred of the back-to-back, four-room minimal dwellings were added a few years later.

My new school was a fairly short walk away, across a large quad in the middle of the housing complex and there were always a few other kids walking toward the school building. I remember little about the second grade other than being excited about learning how to read and to print capital and lower-case letters. An image lingers in my brain of a specific part of the playground which I invariably gravitated to during recesses and eventually even after school. The monkey bars were basic: one low, one middle and one high steel rung attached together in a line. I was hanging by both my knees upside down on the middle bar, in between a slightly older girl trying to do pull-ups on the upper bar and a slightly shorter one trying to get a foot up on the lowest one when I overheard my first conversation about where babies come from. The younger girl said that storks brought babies while the slightly older girl insisted that "babies come out of your mom's butt."

My father and I spent a good deal of time together during the next couple of years. He had started playing golf on the weekends, often with one of my new uncles, and I happily went with him to the course every time I got the chance. He gave me a nickel for every stray ball I found and taught me how to use the crank style, ball-washing machines. I never took up the sport, beyond the miniature kind, as he may have hoped I would, but I was intrigued by the activity, loved being on the golf course and treasured our time together.

The two of usually dyed easter eggs together every year and Daddy hid them in all kinds of interesting places for me to find the next morning. He taught me how to decorate our Christmas tree to in the same way his parents had, using the tree stand and the ornaments he inherited from them. He even had what were then actual aluminum icicles, as they were called, carefully wrapped up in old newspapers. He taught me how to hang these glittering strings one by one starting at the back of each branch of the tree. This was definitely a time-consuming activity yet clearly a satisfying one for my father. I carried that tradition into my own adulthood the first time I lived in a real house with my husband and baby. I used the same icicles in the same way then carefully removed and re-wrapped them each year, as well. I also used same circular tree stand with three large and impossible to replace colored lightbulbs which eventually burned out, and the icicles began to disintegrate. It was a time-consuming activity, to be sure, yet it helped assuage my loneliness during that time in my life, and I always felt my Dad was right there with me.

On the first Fourth of July that we spent together, my father tutored me in the use of firecrackers, "worms," and sparklers, and told me the story of how he nearly lost a finger when he reached for a firecracker that hadn't gone off and it exploded between his fingers. Maybe he was experiencing some regret or guilt about having missed so much of my life up to that point and was making up for lost time, or maybe he really enjoyed being a father. Perhaps it was some of both. Interviewing him not long before his death, I asked Daddy if it had been difficult for him to give up playing music professionally.

> Ken: Sure. When I left the band and moved to Wichita, the feeling was that I wouldn't be in the music business anymore because no one would know me there. Funny thing was that one of the first people I met in Wichita was a musician who'd been in the same place I was in

Florida when I was down there on R & R. He had his own band there. He wanted to use me on weekends for things like the Broadway shows that would come into town. *Hello Dolly* was one, the Shrine Circus, and so on, and of course on New Year's Eve.

Dawn: I remember you taking me with you when you played for the Ice Capades and the Circus, and you turned your saxophone case on its end for me to sit on, so I could be right next to you in the front corner of the band stand. I had a great view. I remember the lion trainer with his long black whip inside of the big wire enclosure with all the big lions. And suddenly his lower arm was bleeding and he quickly pulled out a white handkerchief and wrapped it around his wrist but by the end of the act the blood had seeped through. I always wondered if that was part of the act to make him look braver or a true accident and if the lion got punished because of it.

Ken: I also played at Sims Park in Riverside for their Summer Concert series.

Dawn: Yes, I remember that too, in that white Gazebo! Why did you stop those jobs?

Ken: Well, it got to the point where I just wanted to get rid of everything because if I didn't, I would end up going out on the road again, since most of the music business involved traveling unless you lived in a large city and Ruth wanted to be in Wichita.

In 1947, my stepmother, Ruth Ann, had written the following words underneath the heading, "My Greatest Ambition," on the

page entitled "Wife's Personal Record" in a special book she and my father had received as a wedding gift: "I used to want to be a model. Now that I am married, my greatest ambition would be to be an ideal housewife and mother." The dozens of photographs of Ruth Ann posing as if she were a fashion model, around the time she met my father, are obvious proof of her modeling aspirations (and certainly indicative of the lifelong obsession she had with posing both herself and others for endless snapshots). She would later say more than once that her mother had forbidden her to pursue a career in modeling. Whether Ruth Ann actually believed what she wrote about wanting to be an ideal housewife and mother, or she thought that saying so would please my father, as well as whomever might be reading the book, it was not the way her life would unfold.

In Wichita, Ruth Ann had immediately procured a door-to-door sales job working for a photographer. She not only went from house to house setting up in-home appointments; she also accompanied the photographer when he returned to pose people for their portraits and then returned to show the proofs and make the final sales. She later sold Tupperware for a while before becoming a top salesperson for Encyclopedia Britannica, one of several types of such books sold exclusively door-to-door in the 1950s and 1960s. One of the perks of her *Man of the Year* award was a free set of *Encyclopedia Britannica Jr.* with my name in gold on each volume. I have no doubt that her success at selling things was due in great part to her tenacity and persistence in the art of persuasion. I'm also certain that some people purchased whatever she might be selling in order to get her to stop talking.

Sometime during that first year of our settling in as a family, Ruth Ann was persuaded to join her younger sister and their mother in becoming a member of a conservative, non-denominational church they had been attending. She and I then began going to the same church every Sunday morning for Bible Study followed by worship service, Sunday night services and soon Wednesday night meetings as well. My father and uncle did not share this interest and often played golf on Sunday mornings but my two younger cousins and I had no choice in the matter.

For the next few years, I mostly daydreamed during the sermon part of the church services though I really enjoyed the singing which usually consisted of several hymns before the sermon and a couple more after the sermon. Since no musical instruments were used, the entire congregation sang together in four-part harmony. Ruth Ann loved to sing and she had a beautiful soprano voice. This shared experience brought us closer for a time. It also led to my involvement in choral singing throughout high school, college, and in later life, including the past two decades. There is a growing body of research investigating the psychological and physical benefits of singing in processing trauma , as well as the therapeutic applications of music in the healing of PTSD.

My father was not at home the night a never-to-be-forgotten trauma-laden incident occurred.

> **I am eight years old, sitting at our kitchen table in our duplex eating a bowl of canned peaches after some sort of discussion with my stepmother during which I had disagreed with her. She walks into the kitchen and tells me in a steely voice that she's going to leave me home alone while she goes to church that night because I had "sassed" her.**

Did she really think that missing a Wednesday night, hour-long church service was going to be an effective punishment to correct my behavior or did she actually have some idea of how afraid I was of being left alone in the dark at night and therefore feel it was the best way to discipline me in order to make sure I would never again disagree with anything she might say?

As soon as she leaves, I begin feeling uneasy. The darker it grows, the more anxious I become. I get the idea to telephone the kind woman whom I had spent weekdays with the previous summer. When she answers her phone, I tell her I am alone and begin to cry, admitting I am scared. She assures me that she will be right over and arrives in just a few minutes, pulling the weathered red wagon that I'm familiar with. She tells me to get in the wagon and we quickly cross the grassy quad between our units to the duplex just like ours, where she is raising eight boys whose names I had memorized from the oldest to the youngest: Joe, Tony, Pat, Chris, Jackie, Bede, David and Ray. I have never been in this crowded dwelling at night, or ever seen the boys' father. When we arrive, one of the older boys pulls a younger brother onto his lap to make room for me to sit at the already crowded table. I watch, fascinated, as the strong and sturdy looking Mr. Crawley moves his fingers over a long string of little beads with a pretty little gold cross dangling from the bottom, while everyone else, except the youngest children, repeat the same words over and over. I am surprised to see these often loud, rowdy boys so clean and calm. As this unusual ritual

**comes to an end, Mrs. Crawley takes me into
one of the two bedrooms where I quickly
fall asleep on the big bed next to the baby
in his crib.**

I assume Mrs. Crawley must have left a note for my parents
before taking me to her house that memorable night. I have no way of
knowing what words might have been exchanged when my stepmother
came to get me—whether she was grateful, vexed, or embarrassed.
I was certain she would be angry with me, yet the matter was not
mentioned at all, as if it had never happened.

By the third grade, I was a latchkey kid as we were called at the
time, which meant I was alone after each school day for two or more
hours before either of my parents got home. We didn't yet have a
television or even a radio at that time and Ruth Ann gave me chores
to do daily to pass the time. The tasks included emptying and cleaning
the several ashtrays she and my father used daily and hand-washing
my father's dirty socks. It didn't take that long to complete such things
and eight-year-olds did not have homework in those days. In good
weather, I sometimes sat outside on the porch steps playing with a
young cat who had begun to come around or rode the second-hand
red scooter my father had gotten somewhere and brought home for
me, for short distances around the duplex. This was my first venture
into duplicity, since I had been instructed by my stepmother not to
go out of the house at all during that time. The following year I often
lingered on the playground after school, practicing hanging by both
knees or doing one-knee turnovers on the parallel bars. This minor
deceit was never discovered and, for the first time, I began to feel I
had some small amount of control over my own life.

I was getting close to nine years old when something transpired
that paralleled the traumatic ABCs incident in the hotel room five
years earlier.

**We are standing at a bus stop on a busy street
in the middle of town. Ruth Ann is trying
to teach me the street names and have me**

explain which ones re parallel and which ones intersect. She is giving me information and asking me to repeat it. When I am unable to do what she wants, she becomes progressively cross. My stomach starts to hurt. The bus stops for us but she waves it on. It is getting dark. She begins again, in her slightly louder, irritated voice, "Douglas Street runs east to west!" I don't understand which way is east and which is west. She names another street and asks me which way it runs. I can't tell her. The bus stops again and she waves it on again. She then insists that we are not going home until I can repeat back to her whatever it is she wants me to learn. I can't hold back my tears. I feel smaller and smaller. The sky has darkened. I am cold. The third time the bus stops, she gives me a quick push and we get on. She keeps talking on the bus but I've gone somewhere else, deep inside myself, and I can't hear her.

Years went by before I learned that I was directionally challenged, a condition sometimes referred to as spatial or geographic dyslexia. This affliction is distinguished by a tendency to become disoriented easily, and for some people (like myself) having great difficulty retracing directions or reading maps. A great many other people in the world live with this challenge to one degree or another. We simply do not have an inner compass. To this day, I emerge from a building or an elevator and more often than not, turn in the exact opposite direction of the one I need to be heading in. My husband simply waits patiently for a few moments until I realize I've once again headed in the direction opposite the way I needed to turn.

Around that same time in my childhood, my stepmother decided I should be seeing a dentist. Getting to the dentist's office required a bus trip into town, transferring to another bus and then remembering where to get off. Once I stepped off the bus, I needed to walk a few blocks to a tall building, find the elevator once inside, get off on the correct floor, and locate the dentist's office. It was an anxiety-producing excursion I always dreaded.

Surely Ruth Ann must have gone with me once at least once to show me the steps to getting there and to introduce me to the dentist. Did she do such things all by herself when she was a child? She obviously had no trouble with directions and she seemed to be a spirited person willing to try new things without any fear of failure. Clearly, she simply had no context for understanding how challenging and anxiety producing this particular task was for me.

With or without a parent in the waiting room, I suspect that many people of my generation have less than happy memories about their early dental experiences.

A pretty, dark haired lady tells me her name is June and helps me step onto a stool and into the huge black chair. As she clips a giant white paper bib onto my clothing, she smiles as if to reassure me that I will be okay. A gray-haired man in a white jacket and big glasses appears. He speaks to June in muted, short words, though never to me. When June places big clear goggles on my face, they soon become spattered with various materials so I can't really see much even if I open my eyes. I feel trapped.

When a larger, rubber rimmed mask is placed over my whole face, it was even more disquieting and made me feel woozy and weird. Once released from the mask or the goggles, after the endless mouth rinsing with cold water that required stretching as far as possible to my left side and spitting into the porcelain miniature basin yet again, the paper bib was removed and I would be helped down and out of the chair. June would then smile down at me and give me a little note which I was told to exchange for ice cream in the drugstore on the first floor. Once I made my way to the elevator, down to the first floor and into the drugstore, I always felt incredibly small reaching my arm up to hand the piece of paper to the man behind the counter. Once he noticed me, and figured out that I wasn't attached to an adult, the piece of paper he took from me was quickly exchanged for a frozen fudge bar. I could only tarry so long in the drugstore or standing outside, feeling self-conscious and conspicuous while trying to eat an ice-cold chocolate bar that I didn't really like the taste of, before figuring out how to dispose of the wrapper and stick prior to the equally anxiety producing journey home. This entire ordeal became only slightly easier as I grew older. Even in adulthood, many years passed before I was able to show up on time, without feeling anxious, for any dental appointment, whether it was for a routine cleaning, a filling, a tooth extraction, or a root canal.

That summer, without asking my opinion in the matter, Ruth Ann signed me up for viola lessons. Getting there required an even longer bus trip across town, before climbing some stairs that led to a small attic-like space in an old brick building. After a few days, having found no comfort or inspiration in the small class, I made an impulsive but willful decision to skip the lesson entirely. Instead of transferring to the second bus, I ventured into the big Woolworth's store on that particular corner each day. After getting myself onto one of the red bar stools at the counter I would order a nineteen-cent vanilla malt. I figured out how to remove the change I needed to pay for the malts from a large clear plastic piggy bank my paternal grandparents had given me years before and which had grown nearly full of pennies, nickels, and dimes.

It took some time, using the straw provided, to finish this sweet, thick, concoction which was mixed in a big stainless-steel container. Half of the malt was poured into a footed, V-shaped glass and the other half left in the shiny tall container, from which I would refill the glass. After slowly consuming this deliciously satisfying refreshment,

I'd wander around Woolworth's by myself for a while before getting on the bus and going home. The young man who was teaching the class eventually contacted my stepmother concerning my absences, and my deception was discovered. I believe this was the line I crossed which led to the first belt episode punishment. I will never know how my stepmother made her decisions in regard to the disciplinary methods she chose for me, or if she ever read Dr. Benjamin Spock's bestselling book on Baby and Child Care—first published in 1946— which advised parental affection over corporal punishment, a widely accepted form of discipline in the 1940s and 1950s. What is clear is that my father seemed to relinquish any responsibility whatsoever in the matter, leaving such choices entirely up to his wife.

Clearly Ruth Ann was trying to prove to herself, to my father and to everyone else that she was doing all the right things a good mother should be doing, and physically punishing children for whatever might be deemed bad behavior was used by a high percentage of parents in those times. Debate about both the effectiveness and the effects of physical punishment in childhood seems to continue among some parents even now.

The first time my father took me into my bedroom, shut the door, removed his leather belt and told me he was going to have to punish me, I was clueless as to what was about to happen. I cried as much from the shock of my father's actions as from the stinging pain of the belt strap against my bare skin. The next time this event occurred, I was forewarned after overhearing my stepmother declaring emphatically, "you have to use the belt!" My dad (who I am quite certain never received this type of punishment in his childhood) prefaced the wallops that time by saying rather sadly, "This hurts me as much as it does you." The hard thwack of leather on the exposed skin of my thighs was just as startling, though it seemed to me that my father might be using a little less force than he had before. I cried louder thinking maybe it would make the ordeal end more quickly. After the belt whippings stopped, I convinced myself it was because my father refused to keep delivering such a frightening and painful kind of punishment.

Any time Ruth Ann's job took her out of town overnight, I was always happy to have that special time alone with my father. Ruth Ann had taught me how to prepare a meal on such occasions: put two Russet potatoes in the oven to bake for one hour; fashion two round patties from ground beef then fry them on both sides; and boil some frozen peas. On those evenings, after helping me clean up the dishes, my dad would set up a little table and some folding chairs outside under a large oak tree that stood in the space at the end of our building whenever the weather was nice so we could play games. He taught me how to play Chinese Checkers and introduced me to Scrabble, which became a lifelong pleasure, though it would be a long time before I even came close to my dad's high scores. When it was my bedtime, he always tucked me in, and kissed me goodnight.

I had grown used to calling out to my father in the middle of the night when I had what I'd been told were "growing pains" in my legs. He never failed to come and massage my legs until I fell back asleep. A keen memory of a night when my stepmother was away and he didn't respond when I called out to him has never left me.

I keep calling louder and louder, but Daddy doesn't come. I finally get out of bed to search for him but can't find him anywhere. The light is on in the living room where I see bunch of bed pillows in the corner piled up on top of the telephone. I don't understand. I begin to feel nervous and uneasy. I decide to call my Aunt Fern who tells me not to worry, that she and my uncle will come right over.

When my father returned not long after they arrived, he explained that he'd gone to his musician friend's house to play poker, and had covered our new, corded telephone so that it wouldn't wake me if it rang. He said he hadn't been gone very long.

Did my aunt ever say anything to his wife about that night? Was my father embarrassed to find his brother-and sister-in-law at our house when he came home? Did he tell his wife what happened? Did she think it was fine for him to leave me alone? Did it ever even occur to either of them that I might be afraid of being left alone in the dark at night given what had transpired during my first year of life.

The summer I turned ten, we moved into a three-bedroom brick home in a new housing development. The house had a small screened in porch and a big, undeveloped backyard. My stepmother took me with her to stores where we spent hours sitting on stools in front of a slanted counter that held large sample books of wallpaper, which was a popular house decorating trend in the early 1950s. I was happy though surprised when she said I could help pick out the wallpaper that would go on one wall of my bedroom as well as the paint color for the rest of the walls, although she got the final say, of course. I remember the wallpaper being clusters of flowers in various shades of pink with green leaves on a dark background. My father used the third bedroom in the house to store samples for the advertising company he was working for at the time and continued to work for until his retirement. Someone loaned us an upright piano which fit against one wall of that room and my dream of taking piano lessons came true for a short while.

I was shy at my new school at first. I tried to consume my lunch—a baloney and American cheese on white bread with mayonnaise sandwich, a small bag of potato chips and a couple of store-bought Quaker Oat cookies—as slowly as I possibly could while reading, instead of joining the other kids outside. In time, however, I was lured onto the playground by the Double Dutch jump ropes, and eventually discovered I was also good at tether ball. "Red Rover, Red Rover" became my favorite game because I could run fast and hard and I was good at changing directions at the last second to break through the linked hands.

Ruth Ann's younger sister and family lived only a couple of blocks away from us in their own new house and we spent lots of time with them, especially during the summer months. Possibly because they got a television set before we did, or perhaps because their set was larger, we often walked over to their house on summer evenings to watch TV shows like I *Love Lucy, Ozzie and Harriet,* or *Father Knows Best.* My two cousins and I sat on the floor in front of the television eating freshly popped corn drizzled with melted butter. We drank our Pepsi Colas out of brightly colored aluminum tumblers.

I began to feel comfortable calling Ruth Ann "Mother." My two cousins felt more like a younger sister and brother. During warm weather holidays such as the Fourth of July we three kids helped make home-made ice cream by taking turns cranking my uncle's wooden ice-cream maker handle until it required adult strength to continue. We devoured the vanilla ice cream after the mid-afternoon barbecues, along with generous pieces of my aunt's famously delicious homemade peach pies. We gleefully watched the aerial fireworks display together on July Fourth and often went to drive-in movies together, parking our cars in side-by-side slots, leaving a space in between for lawn chairs for the grownups and blankets for the kids. My cousins would occasionally spend a night at our house, the three of us sleeping together on the floor in the spare bedroom that I liked to think of as the "music room".

My cousins' father, an avid and skilled bowler, took me with him to the bowling alley a few times. I wasn't really inspired to learn to bowl. However, I was totally fascinated with the pin boys—a job for teenage boys that didn't exist past the 1950s—who sat on a ledge behind the pins, jumped down to remove any that were knocked down after the first of two turns before sending the ball back to the bowler and quickly getting their legs out of the way. After the second turn they swiftly put all the pins back in the proper positions and once again sent the ball rolling back to the bowler. My uncle also took me fishing once, though after he discovered I had thrown a still wiggling fish on the pier back into the water, I was not invited again! A distant echo floats back to me—the laughter of children playing tag in the twilight.

I am one of the children. We are chasing each other around on sweet-smelling, freshly-

**mown grass, giggling and carefree, as we
try to catch lightning bugs to hold in our
cupped hands for a minute or two. My legs
are strong, my skin tanned brown as a berry,
as Daddy often exclaims.**

Ruth Ann's older sister and her husband had no children of their
own, whether by choice or by chance I never knew. They gave each
of us kids thoughtful and unique gifts for Christmas, Easter and our
birthdays, and surprise treats like spending the night at their house
or taking us on special outings. Since their house had a basement,
the extended family gathered there when tornado warnings got bad
enough. My cousins and I engaged in "quiet tag" or hide and seek
while the grownups listened to the radio and played card games around
a table in the Southwest corner. We all spent Christmas Eve at their
house every year, and watched the New Year's Day parade there also.
After the parade, the three sisters habitually retreated to the kitchen
while the men watched the football game, and we cousins entertained
ourselves in various ways. My life began to feel predictable and safe.

Not long after my eleventh birthday, I sensed something was
amiss when my father wasn't home on Saturday morning and a Western
Union telegram was delivered to our front door. My mother read it
and said nothing though her energy and demeanor quickly changed.
She seemed preoccupied and distracted. Another knock on the front
door brought a Special Delivery letter that night. The minute Mother
left for work Monday morning, I quickly found the telegram, which
simply read: "SPECIAL DELIVERY LETTER WILL REACH YOU
EARLY THIS EVENING LOVE KENNETH."

The typewritten letter that had arrived that evening began,
Dear Ruth . . .

There comes a time when a person has got to do what
they feel they must do. I would rather cut off my arm

than do what I'm about to but that wouldn't help. I am leaving Wichita. I realize this will put many hardships on your shoulders and that I am causing a great deal of suffering but if I stay there seems no hope for me. I want to get away by myself and try to grow up again. I must start from scratch and by myself. As for Dawn, I think the only thing to tell her is the truth, that I have gone to try and get a fresh start.

Reading the letter, all I could think of was that my father had left me and I felt as if I'd been struck by lightning. He ended his communication saying, "Please have faith in my honest intentions. Love, Ken." I carefully put the telegram and letter back in the exact same way I'd found them before I went into shock. I was heartbroken, anxious and panicking. I couldn't let Mother know I'd read the telegram and letter of course, so I had to pretend, just as she was pretending, that everything was normal. All she said to me when I asked was that my father had to go out of town for a few days—something to do with work—and I was forced to keep all my feelings and fears locked inside. It would be over sixty years before I found and read the other two handwritten letters my father sent from the road that summer, containing revelations that would have confused me even more at the age I was then. In his next message to Mother, my father wrote,

> I do hope you understand why I had had to leave the way I did. I am not running away but I am simply doing, something I probably should have done when I left the band.

It becomes obvious that his crisis has at least something to do with becoming dependent on his wife financially rather than her depending on him, which, although he doesn't use the actual words, made him feel emasculated. He talks about needing to overcome a weakness in himself that he seems helpless against. He says that he has "harbored suicidal thoughts at times" when he became "disgusted and ashamed and despondent over my lack of will power."

> This getting away from it all is not an escape, only something I had to do to find myself for myself. It would take a good psychiatrist to figure it all out. But I must stop lying cheating and living two lives in my mind and I can't do it when I'm home.

My dad then urges his wife to think of his absence "as though I have decided to move myself and family to a different location and that naturally a husband might precede his family by a short time–as many men have done."

In the next paragraph, he says "there is no point listing the lies of the recent past" before telling Mother to make a couple of phone calls in regard to band concerts he's supposed to be playing for, and say that he is out of town on an emergency. He ends the letter saying, "I am sick at heart at what I've caused. I will write every day and hope for the best" before ending with "All my love, Ken."

I am deeply saddened when reading this letter, written when my father was thirty-five years old. The line in which he confesses to harboring suicidal thoughts jumps out at me like a flashing neon sign. I was a few years younger than he was when I felt that surely ending my life was the only way out of the guilt and shame I was feeling so deeply at that time. I'm also jolted by his words, "lies of the recent past," which make it clear that my father was not only capable of lying to his wife, but that he had been doing so for a long time. The falsehoods he is referring to seem to be about money, though perhaps there were lies about other things as well?

In his last letter, written from Salt Lake City, my dad describes how attractive he finds the layout of the town before revealing how much he dislikes living in Kansas.

> I wish you could have been here to enjoy the sights. feel certain of one thing, Ruth, I never want to live in flat Kansas again. Of course, sometimes we must do

what we don't want to, but if it's possible, give me the
hills & mountains & water.

The phrase "I never want to live in flat Kansas again" seemed to
imply that he might never return. Though my father came back to our
home about two weeks later, it felt like an eternity to me at the time.

In the black and white snapshots from the next couple of years,
the three of us look like a normal, happy family. Our summer vacations
took us from horseback riding in Colorado to the Carlsbad Caverns
in New Mexico and, one year, all the way to California. Seatbelts
had yet to be invented and I had the back seat of the car to stretch
out in anytime I felt like it. My father and mother often drove all
night, taking turns— to save money on motels I now realize—while I
slept. When they were both awake, presumably assuming that I could
sleep through anything, they would often laugh while singing sweet
or amusing songs I'd never heard before, though I've remembered a
couple of them, such as "The Riddle Song," my entire life.

The two of them driving together for long hours and singing
together to help themselves stay awake I'm guessing was likely
reminiscent of their time crisscrossing the country with the band.
It clearly put them in a good mood. Their affectionate laughter and
duets, combined with the rhythm of the road, made me feel happy,
safe and secure.

During our visit to California, my father drove the three of us
down to the place where he and Ruth Ann had met at Mission Beach
in San Diego. From there he continued driving into Mexico, which
was then an easy crossing, without passports or questions. My father
seems especially relaxed and happy during that vacation.

Back home, the little tufts of grass we'd planted when the house
was new had joined together to form even, green lawns. Daddy bought
a croquet set and taught me how to play. A stray yellow cat we named
Butter adopted us which pleased my mother greatly. Daddy brought
home a German Shepherd puppy one day, naming him Blitz. He

trained him to come when he whistled a special three-note sound created just for him. He was the dog my dad had long wanted, and who would soon become my best friend.

When Blitz dug up some purple petunia's we had planted in the brick enclosed, raised flower bed attached to the front of the  house, Mother was so angry she called our local newspaper and placed an ad to give him away. I figured out how to call the next day, pretending to be her and cancelled the ad. I never knew if Mother complained to the paper about the ad not appearing or just kept complaining to my Dad about the dog.

A few months later, with her younger sister driving the car, we were rushing Mother, moaning in agony in the back seat, to the hospital emergency room where she was diagnosed with what was then referred to as a tubular pregnancy. I never discovered if there was no chance of her getting pregnant after that or if the doctor told her that it would be too dangerous to try. I know, from a number of references in their letters to each other, that she and my father had hoped and planned to have what she always referred to as "a child of their own."

I can well imagine now that having to let go of the dream of having her own baby with my father must have been devastating and depressing to Mother and extremely disappointing to Daddy as well. To have that desire thwarted most likely impacted their relationship and influenced their future in all sorts of ways. I wonder how different my life might have been if Daddy's dream of "starting the family" had come to fruition? Is it possible that she and daddy would have stayed together? How might that have changed all our lives?

After witnessing several other young people in the congregation nearing their teens dutifully take the plunge at church, I felt compelled during the invitational song after the sermon one Sunday morning, to walk all the way to front row of the church building and sit down as a sign that I wanted to be baptized. The ritual began with the minister taking my hands in his and asking me something like "Do you accept Jesus Christ as your Lord and Savior?" After I said "I do", he directed me toward the door leading to the baptistry and some female member of the congregation came in to help me get undressed and into the long white baptismal garment before guiding me to the steps into the water to meet the minister. I suppose that same lady then opened the curtains to the baptistry so that everyone present could watch this ritual. As I stood in what for me was waist high water the preacher positioned me, raised his right hand and proclaimed "I now baptize thee in the name of the Father, the Son and the Holy Ghost" before submerging me in the water. When he raised me up out of the water, removing the cloth he had held over my nose and mouth, I felt cleansed, purified, and newly protected by God. I believed that all my sins were washed away and I was saved, though in truth I didn't really understand what any of that meant. What sins had I committed? Was I now assured of going to Heaven, whatever or wherever that was? Was everybody who hadn't been baptized going to Hell to experience fire and brimstone for eternity? It was a concept I really never could quite grasp.

One reward for completing this rite of passage was finally getting to taste the freshly baked unleavened bread supplied by the church ladies, and picking up my own little cup for a sip of grape juice when the silver communion trays were passed down the rows of pews on Sunday morning. An additional baptismal bonus was being welcomed into the Young People's Class that met before church services every Sunday evening. Becoming part of the church's teenage group gave me access to shared activities such as the monthly skating rink nights, autumn hayrides, and other special outings which gave me a previously unexperienced feeling of inclusion and acceptance. My bonds with the young people in that community continued to grow during the church-sponsored summer sleep-away camps I attended in Arkansas.

By the time I was fourteen, I had experienced my first kiss and a few more. My interest in the opposite sex was quickly expanding, though nothing beyond kissing and what was then called "necking," had yet to take place. In the meantime, my parents' arguments were increasing both in frequency and in noise level. Every once in a while, I was awakened in the middle of the night by the sound of Mother's disgruntled voice growing louder by the minute. My father's more measured and subdued voice would break in occasionally. One memorable night, he grabbed a blanket and a pillow, locked himself in the bathroom, and slept in the bathtub until morning. Every time that memory arises, I wonder what would have happened if I'd needed to use the bathroom in the middle of the night? Before long, Daddy began spending more time out of town, perhaps because his job demanded it, though it must surely have been partly to break away from his wife's persistent, preachy nagging and their continuous bickering.

I eventually realized that once Mother bit into a subject or began trying to persuade someone of her opinion about anything, it was as if she literally could not stop talking or persisting in presenting her particular viewpoint. The person she was talking to would begin to feel badgered. She didn't seem to have the ability to consider, much less accept, any point of view that differed from her own.

Ruth Ann no longer counted on my father to mete out any punishment she deemed I deserved or needed in order to "teach me a lesson." If her criticism and belittling failed to elicit some kind of response from me, she would grab both of my forearms and begin vigorously trying to shake some sense into me, as she put it. Her long fingernails digging into the backs of my arms would often break the skin. If she was particularly upset, she would slap me across the face. This stinging rebuke caused my nose to bleed a few times which, oddly perhaps, only served to make me feel more defiant. I always stifled my anger, never yelling back, just seething silently while my resentment against her continued to build. I was unaware that my anger, as well as the sadness that lay underneath, was sinking deeper and deeper into my subconscious, and wouldn't begin to rise to the surface slowly over the years to come.

I had stolen an insignificant small toy a couple of times, for no particular reason that I was actually aware of, from Woolworth's during one of my secret stopovers in that store. My duplicitous behavior continued and became more artful during the next few years. My dishonesty continued in other behaviors such as secretly wearing one of Mother's blouses to school, then returning it to same spot before she got home, or putting rocks in the bottom of the bucket I was supposed to be filling with dandelion weeds so that it looked as if I'd completed the task. The first time Mother discovered that I had turned on our black and white TV while she wasn't there, you'd have thought I'd killed the cat. After that I always set a box of frozen peas on the top of the flat-topped set while watching American Bandstand. By moving the peas around every few minutes and taking it off at just the right time before turning the TV off, it wouldn't be warm if Mother decided to run her hand across its top.

From a psychological perspective, I now understand that feelings of inadequacy, low self-esteem, and not being "good enough" are known to sometimes lead to deceptive behaviors such a lying as well as stealing, both of which can provide a fleeting sense of power and control over one's life.

The more exasperated Mother became with my father and with her inability to bend things to her will in regard to him, the more she took her frustration out on me. She began trying desperately to shape my behavior. I didn't perceive at the time, of course, that she was desperate to control something because she was beginning to feel her life with my father falling apart.

With both of my parents preoccupied, neither one was available to help me with homework of any kind. I was floundering in my Junior High Algebra class, getting further and further behind in my lack of understanding when I finally got up my nerve to ask the teacher for help. He told me to come see him after school. He was tall with short brown hair, fairly young, and self-assured. I felt a bit intimidated by him. As I stood in front of his desk and I tried to explain my dilemma, instead of asking specific questions or offering to help me, all I remember is him smiling at me, then getting up from behind his desk, walking over and putting his arm around me and squeezing my shoulders which made me feel confused and uncomfortable. I felt near tears and he just hugged me harder, which gave me a yucky feeling. He never addressed the problem or helped me in any way. He then gave me a D- in the class. My father was fairly upset and perplexed, yet didn't invite any further conversation about it. I don't think I told him about asking the teacher for help. I just felt embarrassed, ashamed and saddened to have disappointed him.

Looking back on that experience, though I don't remember anything beyond the math teacher's repeated hug occurring, I believe there was a seductive, flirtatious quality to his actions which would definitely be considered inappropriate in our current times. I was fortunate that he didn't do anything more.

My most rebellious act, perhaps, came in the spring of that year. Having helped decorate the gym for the ninth-grade sock hop and knowing that the boy I had a crush on would be there fueled my determination to go to the dance in outright defiance of my mother who, despite my reasoned arguments and outright pleading, had remained firmly against it. The church taught that all actions and even all thoughts were either good or bad. Any kind of dancing was considered a sin. I did not understand why dancing would send me to Hell. The only explanation I ever heard had something to do with impure thoughts.

When the night for the dance arrived, I calmly walked out of the house when Mother was in another room, then ran the few blocks to my best friend's house, zigzagging behind trees and through backyards—most were unfenced in those days—scared that Mother would show up at any moment. My friend's mother, feeling sympathy for me, quickly drove us both to the school.

I see Mother's car pulling up to the front of the building just as we are going inside and I promptly dash into the girl's bathroom.

Before I can hide in one of the stalls, she comes marching in—furious—to confront me. There are a couple of other girls in the room, which is likely what keeps her from forcibly dragging me out. After a quick hissed, clenched jaw lecture, she tells me in no uncertain terms to come to the car, then turns abruptly and leaves, clearly expecting me to follow her. I ignore her completely, turn the other way, and rush into the gym towards the sound of the Everly Brothers. As soon as it becomes clear that Mother has decided against coming into a large room full of students and teachers and making a scene, I relax.

Feeling exhilarated after I managed to almost master the jitterbug that night, I had no impure thoughts. A bunch of ninth-graders and some of their teachers spent a few hours in a gymnasium having fun; what was bad or sinful about that? The freedom to move my body in time to music seemed liberating in some fundamental way. It would be over two years, however, before I would attend another dance and by that time I was living in a different city, with a new stepmother.

Did Mother leave the front door unlocked on purpose and shut herself in her bedroom so she wouldn't have to see me when I came back home that night? Was she angry or depressed or both because my father wasn't there? Did she ever tell him what I had done? I experience a surge of compassion. I can envisage how utterly unhappy and defeated she must have been feeling as she began to realize that she couldn't even control me, let alone my father, any longer.

So many things could have gone wrong the Saturday night I crawled out my bedroom window, after putting pillows and clothes under the covers to make it look as if I was still there. The neighborhood friend who had suggested this mischief did the same and met me in the middle of the deserted street at midnight. As she had arranged, a car drove up and we quickly hopped into it with a couple of boys she knew who may or may not have been old enough to drive, and who may or may not have been drunk, or as I realize now, at least "high" on something. In reality, they seemed more interested in boasting and showing off than in any hands-on interaction with us. As I remember it, they just drove way faster than they should have, careening around the streets in the neighborhood for a while before finally stopping back at the spot where they'd picked us up and quickly speeding away, guffawing loudly. My friend and I parted and each of us managed to crawl back through the windows into our homes and beds without detection.

A few months later, my father drove me to the church building to drop me off for the Young People's Meeting before the Sunday evening service. We were early, which I'm sure he had planned. After parking the car, Daddy turned to me and said he had something he wanted to tell me. He then stated calmly that he was leaving Ruth Ann. He confided that he was seeing someone else, adding quite matter-of-factly that they were not engaged in a sexual relationship but that he cared very much for her. I wasn't shocked. I couldn't blame him for choosing not be with Mother, or for wanting to be with someone else. In that moment, I was happy for him.

When my father mentioned that he was going to be moving to another town, a couple of hours away, I was taken aback and immediately felt anxious. As what he was saying began to sink in, I literally begged him to take me with him. He began patiently explaining why that wouldn't work, since he was basically a traveling salesman. He said he couldn't leave me alone for days at a time. I was devastated, and adamant that I did not want to live alone with Mother. I even told my father about the shaking and face slapping, and showed him the scars on the backs of my forearms. I'm guessing he may have anticipated my reaction as my father clearly had an ace up his sleeve.

He offered me a solution I was okay with—enrolling me in a small high school situated on the campus of a Christian college in Arkansas. Having met a couple of kids at the summer church camp who had spoken about this school and, seeing it as an escape from the palpable distress and uncertainty surrounding me, I was actually quite eager to go. The most emotional part for me was leaving our dog, Blitz. I hadn't anticipated missing him quite so fiercely and sometimes cried myself to sleep thinking about him. I was broken-hearted a couple months later when I was told that he had bitten someone and had to be put to sleep.

Was that story actually true? Mother never wanted a dog and she never bonded with Blitz. Is it possible that with both my father and me gone she just didn't want to take care of a dog she never really liked, or wanted around? Is it possible that Blitz, in his misery, became aggressive? How would he have gotten out of the fenced backyard? I experience a sudden burst of anger toward my father. What was he possibly thinking by abandoning the dog we both loved when he left Ruth Ann? How could he have left Blitz with a woman who didn't love him, who would just see him as a burden and as a reminder of my father's and my absence? Did my father make any effort at all to find a new home for him?

I was relieved to be on my own, so to speak, at the HS Academy on the college campus. I made new friends. The dorm rules and curfews were clear and seemed reasonable. I enjoyed a math class for the first and only time in my life due to the skill, kindness and patience of the female teacher. After I was hit in the head with a ball while trying to learn to play softball, my Physical Education teacher, somehow knowing I liked roller skating, suggested that I do that in the small wooden gymnasium during the hour-long class instead. I was greatly relieved. As I reflect on that time in my life, I believe those hours of circular rhythmic movement by myself became an important meditative practice for me during those spring months.

Several students ended up at the Academy that year due to the desegregation crisis in Little Rock, although at the time I had very limited awareness regarding what was happening. I was truly oblivious to what was going on in the rest of the world. We had no access to newspapers or magazines or television news casts. I had no clue that desegregation efforts in the south were being met with impassioned resistance, about the historical significance of "The Lost Year" or of the impact Orval Faubus had on the civil rights movement.

At some point in that school year, all the students were required to go to a building on the college campus to watch a movie. At age fifteen, I was incredibly naive and uneducated regarding communism, The Red Scare, The Cold War, politics or world history in general. I had no idea the president of the college was a well- known crusader against communism or a staunch member of the John Birch Society. The main thing I remember about that unnerving film is watching the blood-red color slowly moving across a map of the United States like spilled ink and the dire warning that communism would take over the world by a specific date. I recall calculating that I would be in my early twenties at that time. Having gotten the message that communism was going to make everyone very poor, I imagined myself having to search for enough food to feed the children I must have assumed I would have by that age.

Only recently have I begun to reflect on the fact that at that time I was living in a politically and religiously conservative isolated community, or to comprehend how deeply the persistent dogma that I'd been exposed to during the previous decade was embedded in my psyche. The new environment provided me with a feeling of security and safety in many ways, and yet it was a form of fundamentalist religious ideology that limited my knowledge and understanding of the larger world around me. It stunted my ability to think logically, critically, or independently.

Seven

The Phone Call, The Meeting, and a Visitation

Life will give us whatever experience is most helpful for the evolution of our consciousness.

~ Eckhart Tolle

Nothing ever goes away until it has taught us what we need to know.

~ Pema Chödrön

After being back in Kansas with my father and his new wife for the summer, and spending a few wonderful weeks on a road trip with my grandparents and cousin to visit other cousins in Michigan, I very much wanted to return to the boarding school in Arkansas and be with the friends I'd made there. My father told me he couldn't afford to send me back. I tried everything I could think of to try and persuade him, and he told me that nothing I said could change his mind.

Was it truly a money issue or is it possible that my father was still trying to build the family he'd always dreamed of and wanted me to be part of that? Or could it possibly even be partly that he had simply missed spending more time with me?

My newest stepmother seemed very interested in treating me well. She had primary custody of her two young daughters and I welcomed the new experience of being a big sister. When I was asked to the fall homecoming dance in the large public high school I was then attending, my step-mother designed and sewed a beautiful dress for me to wear to the dance and tutored me in how to slow dance, which I'd never done.

The drama teacher/director at my new high school, perhaps happy to have an enthusiastic new thespian, or perhaps sensing the anxiety beneath my outward appearance, seemed eager to help me feel welcome in any way she could. Becoming part of the fifty-person A Cappella Chorus, and being cast in the theater department's fall production, gave me instant friends among the two thousand plus students in the school. The opportunities that presented themselves in this expanded environment soon diminished my disappointment about not returning to the small private high school in Arkansas and helped greatly in building my self-confidence. My junior year was overflowing with rehearsals, activities and honors I had never dreamed of receiving as I threw myself into as many new projects as possible, becoming president of the Thespian Society, working on the school newspaper, getting elected secretary of the senior class and so on. In addition, I was lucky enough to be "going steady" with a talented, cute, funny boy my same age who was respectful enough to stop short of "going all the way" in our make-out sessions.

The following year, my drama teacher wrote me an effusive college recommendation letter—giving me a copy of it with the proviso that I not show it to anyone other than my parents—in an effort to obtain a scholarship for me from the Drama Department at the University of Kansas. When I received the scholarship, albeit a bit smaller than I had hoped for, I was thrilled. However, unbeknownst to me, the minister at the church I had been attending on Sundays who had come to see me playing the part of Azuri in *The Desert Song*, wrote to a close friend of his who was the Choral Director and music teacher at a small, two-year Christian college in Nebraska. I have no idea what he said to that teacher that resulted in me receiving a letter in the mail offering me a full drama scholarship for tuition, room and board to that school. Though flattering in a certain way, it didn't alter my desire to attend the nearby University where a number of my friends were planning to go. My father then told me that he needed me to go to the smaller college because he couldn't afford to send me to the University, adding that if I would just attend the college in Nebraska for that year, he would send me anywhere I wanted to go the following year.

This rather duplicitous promise from my father was clearly based on his certainty that I would not want to change schools the following year. Was he really that broke or in debt at the time? Did he have other reasons for wanting me further away. Did he see me going to college at all as just a way to find a husband?

Working full time as a sales clerk at Macy's Department Store that summer, earning money to contribute to my education, had no effect in my efforts to change my father's mind and so I eventually, and somewhat grudgingly, gave up trying to dissuade him. When I was just a few short weeks away from boarding a train to travel to a town I had never seen to begin my first year of college, I happened to be near the telephone when it rang and picked up the receiver.

"Hello."
"Is this Dawn?"
"Yes."
"Dawn, this is your mother."

My stepmother who was watching from the kitchen a few feet away, pregnant with her and my father's soon to be born son, would later say she saw my face turn white as I sank into the small chair next to the telephone and she knew I was in shock. I remember nothing else of that conversation although, clearly, the low-voiced woman on the other end of the phone line said something about wanting to meet me, and I presumably expressed a similar interest. She mentioned driving to Kansas City, saying she would be bringing her son.

Around the time of my seventeenth birthday, shortly before the startling phone call, I had asked my father, "Do you think my birth mother ever thinks about me? Do I look anything like her?" I'm uncertain what effect my questions had on my father or even how he answered them. I did not know that following my query he had decided to look into my birth mother's current whereabouts, explicitly stating—he told me after her phone call—that she was not to contact me.

Several weeks later, my father drove me to the motel where Penny had checked in with her twelve-year-old-son. I have no recollection as to why I decided to dress up for this meeting, or what words, if any, might have been exchanged between me and my dad during that drive.

When we entered the motel room, I encountered a slim, dark-haired woman, slightly shorter than I was. Her eyes were brown, like mine, and I couldn't help but notice the similarities in our facial structure. We were both wearing brownish sheath-style dresses as well as the same color and style high-heeled shoes. I noticed a book on the motel bed with the same title as one I had recently begun reading. I remember thinking, in those first few awkward moments when time seemed to stand still, that I was in the presence of both my parents for the first time in my life that I was conscious of.

What must it have been like for Daddy seeing Penny again? Was he able to detach from whatever emotions he must surely have been experiencing and just remain cordial and calm the way he so often seemed to in other situations? Or was he simply ignoring or repressing what he might have actually been feeling?

My father and I were introduced to the thin, blond-haired boy in the room. My half-brother seemed somewhat timid, or perhaps it was apprehension I sensed in him. My father soon excused himself and left so there was one less person in the hotel room. I think he may have told me beforehand that he was going to do that. Looking back on it, I'm sure he felt my nervousness, and was trying to protect me from too much emotional overload. He may have also been protecting himself. I'm guessing he had a cup of coffee and a cigarette in some nearby cafe. I don't have any idea how long I stayed in the hotel room that first day or what conversations may have ensued. I'm fairly certain that I was, at least partially, mentally and emotionally numbed out.

I do remember going with my newfound mother and brother to a local swimming pool the next day, and attending an AA meeting that evening. I suppose Penny must have mentioned how many years she'd been sober and why she didn't want to miss an Alcoholics Anonymous meeting. By that time, I had some vague understanding that her drinking had played a part in her abandonment of me. I had zero experience, however, with alcohol and was completely ignorant about alcohol addiction. The recitations, declarations, and confessions during the meeting, which included close to a couple dozen men and women of varying ages sitting on foldout chairs, reminded me a bit of going to church, with caffeinated coffee and glazed donuts substituting for Sunday communion of grape juice and unleavened bread.

A few months later, during my December break from college classes, I was both excited and nervous as I stepped onto a commercial airplane for the first time in my life, and flew to Florida to visit my birth mother and my half-brother in their suburban home in Miami. I presume Penny instigated the visit and must have paid for the plane ticket. Meeting Penny's then wheelchair-bound mother, who was living with her daughter and grandson, I had the impression that she was a woman who once had a large personality and a commanding presence but now found herself diminished and resented it deeply. Seemingly completely uninterested in any interaction with me, she mostly confined herself to her room in the house during my fairly short visit.

Penny invited several people into her home for the purpose of meeting me: a best friend from AA, a few neighbors, and a man wearing a clerical collar whom she was clearly very fond of and seemed to be wanting to impress. They all seemed extremely happy to meet me. I felt a bit as if I was being put on display like a new doll or toy.

Did Penny think we were just going to go forward as a loving mother and daughter who found each other after nearly twenty years, as if our separation had nothing to do with her? Despite my father's explicit instructions that she was not to contact me, did the person he contacted perhaps show her the letter in order to let her know her that her daughter was looking for her and wanted to meet her? Or, is it possible she had prayed for this miracle which then seemed to be happening?

On my last night there, Penny drove her son and me to the very swanky Boca Raton Country Club for dinner so she could introduce me to her brother. She had told me with obvious pride that he was the manager there. He didn't actually take a seat and eat with us but stopped by our table to sit with us for a short time, then came back to say goodbye later. He presumably paid for the meal or perhaps there was no charge. I remember him as handsome and extremely cordial. Penny clearly adored him. It seemed as if Penny and I both had some desire at that point to forge a relationship with one another although I can't remember any truly authentic conversations of any depth during that visit.

I was a bit surprised when Penny decided to come to my wedding in 1963. I had two other mothers already in town for the occasion, although my father's current wife was, of course, the official mother of the bride that day. Weddings were much simpler events back then, at least in a small college town in Nebraska. As it turned out—each mother thinking another was helping me perhaps—I put on my wedding dress by myself in my dorm room and then holding the bottom of the dress off the ground, carefully walked the two blocks to the church building. Penny happened to show up in the church basement just as our volunteer photographer was about to take a picture of me. She introduced herself to him as my mother and, likely seeing the resemblance, he quickly posed her behind me as if she was helping me with my dress.

Six months later, my husband gave up a few days when he would normally be studying during a break in his classes to drive us from the town in central Texas where we were living to a very nice mobile home park in Florida where my retired fraternal grandparents lived. They had been unable to come to our wedding and were eager to meet their new grandson-in-law. It was always a great joy for me to spend time with my grandparents, who had been the most consistently stabilizing influence in my life up to that point. After a sweet but short stay with them, we drove to where Penny and my half-brother were living, for an even shorter visit, before driving back to Texas.

We went to a restaurant to have breakfast with them and my husband later told me that he noticed my teen-age brother quickly grab some money from the open cash register drawer as we were leaving. During the next few years, Penny and I exchanged newsy letters occasionally. I signed mine "Love, Dawn." She signed hers, "Love always, Always Love" and at the bottom of at least one, "Your Loving Mother." When our first child was born, I believe my husband must have called her to let her know. She sent a telegram saying, "So glad your ordeal is over."

The word she chose to use in reference to giving birth, and each of the synonyms for that word—nightmare, misery, torture, torment, agony, hell on earth—seems to emphasize what she considered my birth to be. The word "ordeal" didn't then nor has it ever resonated in the least with me. In fact, in my experience of giving birth to three children it has been quite the opposite.

Penny also mailed me a package containing three hand-knit (by herself or by a friend, I never knew) wool soakers which were meant to be worn over a baby's diaper. They were pretty and unusual although, naive as I was at the time, they seemed so impractical that I never used them. They still remain neatly arranged in the square white box they arrived in.

By 1974, my husband and I had separated, and I was with our two children in northern California in order to attend graduate school. Penny's mother had died and she and I had fallen somewhat out of touch. While our children were with their father that summer, I caught a ride to the central east coast with friends and then arranged a short flight to Florida to see Penny and the man she had been living with for a number of years. When they picked me up at the airport, one of the first things Penny said was, "You don't mind if we make a quick stop to have a drink, do you?" The sudden realization that a confirmed alcoholic was no longer sober was a bolt from the blue and disconcerting to say the least. Caught totally by surprise, I immediately began to feel uneasy as well as trapped in a situation I had no idea how to handle. I went into mental auto pilot mode while hiding my feelings inside a facade of equanimity. I have no recall of what kind of or how many drinks Penny and her partner ordered, what I might have been sipping on or how long we remained in the establishment where they had chosen to stop before getting back in the car.

As we reached the area where Penny and her partner lived, I noted that their trailer home seemed somewhat remote, with only a few other mobile homes nearby, and that they were surrounded by a large parcel of land bordered on the back side by a forested area. The three of us ate dinner together in the rather cramped space. I believe wine appeared with the meal. I remained smiling and polite. Blaming my tiredness on jet lag, although I had not, in fact, come from a different time zone, I went to bed in their small guest bedroom as early as I could manage.

Awakened an hour or so later by a heated argument which seemed to be getting physical, between two apparently intoxicated people, I overheard Penny say accusingly, "Are you saying you think my daughter is better than my son?" and her companion answering, "No, I just said she seems like a nice girl." The voices became muffled for a few moments, and then I distinctly heard the word "gun." Unnerved, I quickly dressed and slipped out of the side door of the trailer. Seeing a light on in the nearest mobile home adjacent to theirs I took refuge with the understanding young couple who answered my knock. When I explained why I was there, they told me that their neighbors were both "really nice people, except when they get drunk," before confirming that they did indeed own a gun which had been shot at least once that they were aware of. They invited me stay the rest of the night with them, ushering me to a cushioned platform bed in the back of the trailer where I could look out the window and keep watch on the trailer I had escaped from. I slept very little. There was no way to avoid returning to Penny and her mate's trailer the next morning. I knocked gently and someone said, "Come in." The first thing I noticed was that Penny had bruises forming around one eye and that her companion had several deep scratches on one side of his face. The three of us sat in mostly awkward silence waiting for my half-brother, who was driving from another part of the state with his young family in order to see me. The obvious "elephant in the room" loomed large but was never addressed.

My half-brother arrived, later than expected, which seemed to annoy his mother. His wife appeared shy and slightly uncomfortable, or maybe just very tired. She had a cute baby in her arms and a sweet little girl who looked to be around three or four years old. I'm not certain how I acquired a few snapshots I have from that day. In the one of me with Penny, neither of us is smiling. I look stunned, taciturn, and like I might be sick at any moment. She looks resigned or possibly a bit defiant. Our physical resemblance, however, is unmistakable. The neighbors who had provided me solace the night before had also offered to drive me to the airport, and no one objected. I remained dazed for a good while. I have no memory of getting on the airplane or disembarking wherever it landed.

In late December of 1976, I flew from California to Kansas City and my father then drove himself and me to Florida to see Penny, who was in the hospital dying of lung cancer. He and I talked about all kinds of things during that drive, except the fact that the first woman he had loved and married, the woman who had given birth to me, was nearing death. And, of course, we had no clue that he himself would die from the same disease only thirteen years later.

Seeing the woman who had carried me inside her body for nine months and brought me into this world emaciated and tinged with death at the age of fifty-six was disquieting, and it elicited a wave of compassion in me. The oxygen tent canopied over the top half of her bed meant that she had to lift up the side and stick her head out to speak. She asked for some caviar shortly after we arrived, which her son dutifully went off to try to locate for her while my father likely went off in search of coffee. Finding myself alone in the room with Penny for a brief period, and cognizant of the fact that I most likely would never have the chance again, I asked her if she remembered anything in particular about my birth. I wrote down her response in a journal I was keeping at the time. She said,

> I was knocked out for the last five or six hours and I didn't see you until you were six hours old. I don't think that's a good way to give birth. I think it takes away from the love a mother should feel for her child.

Years later, a friend pointed out that the woman who birthed me seemed to be blaming the medical facility or her doctor for her failure to bond with me. However, her words appeared to be the only apology I was ever going to get and I decided to take them as such. She gave birth to her son five years after I was born, presumably under different and better circumstances, since it seemed as if she had bonded with him from the beginning.

When Penny's physician appeared, and I introduced myself to him in the hallway, he said to me, "What does she have against you?" Taken aback, and wondering what had provoked his question, I responded with the only answer that came to me in that moment. "Her own guilt, I guess," I replied, mentioning that she had abandoned me when I was just over a year old. He said nothing more, and I didn't see him again. I recall little else about that somewhat surreal time except that saying goodbye, knowing this was the last time I would ever be in the presence of the woman who had helped give me life, produced a flood of emotion from some deep, primordial place in me.

A few weeks later, during the night or very early morning, of January 10, 1977, something occurred that was vividly visual, palpable, and utterly galvanizing.

Penny appears at the foot of my bed. She is wearing a long white garment made of gauzy material. It looks like something between

a wedding dress and a nightgown. Her countenance is distraught. She looks confused and somewhat angry. I sit straight up in my bed, looking directly at her. I am captivated by her presence and by her appearance so close and clear. Both her arms are stretched out in front of her as if to show me the double row of heavy looking iron chains hanging from her wrists. I feel sad for her. I feel tears wetting my face as I say out loud, "I forgive you." I repeat this several times, "I forgive you. I forgive you." I watch the shackles loosen, and the chains drop slowly, soundlessly to the floor. Her face begins to soften slightly as her image slowly fades from my view.

I was surprised yet grateful for this unexpected encounter, and for the fact that Penny had been able to contact me as she transitioned out of her body. Her shackled appearance made me realize what a heavy burden of guilt she must have been carrying her entire life regarding her failure, or her inability to give me the care I needed and deserved as an infant. Something seemed to shift for me as I kept assuring her that I forgave her. I thought at the time, naively, that this interaction had settled the matter of her abandonment of me. However, it would be a good many years before that resolution would occur.

A few hours later, Penny's son called to tell me his mother had died, which of course I already knew. I didn't tell him about her "visitation," though I made some reference about a feeling I had in regard to her having left her body. After a moment of silence between us, I commented that she'd had a pretty hard life, to which he quickly replied, "Well, she held it together long enough to raise me." I was at a loss as to how to reply to his statement. He and I communicated a few times shortly after that. However, both of us were in the midst of busy lives, raising children, and living on separate coasts. We eventually lost touch, and have never seen each other again, nor has he responded to my efforts to contact him.

Eight

Ramifications and Reverberations

The consequences of childhood trauma can be widespread and contain hidden symptoms that may remain dormant, accumulating over years or even decades.

~ Peter A. Levine

I didn't realize how attached I was to having somebody else confirm me as being okay. In other words, it didn't come from inside me. It came from someone else's view of me.

~ Pema Chödrön

"Have you ever been raped?"

"Well, no," I replied slowly, "not really, though I have had nonconsensual sex a few times."

"Dawn, nonconsensual sex is rape!"

"Well, I never had a gun to my head or a knife to my throat." The loved one who had asked me the question seemed perplexed and astounded by my answer before repeating the words with greater emphasis: "Nonconsensual sex *is* rape!"

Many years ago, a wise friend said to me, "Oh Dawn, you give up your power so easily." I didn't really grasp what she meant at the time. However, in retrospect, I have come to understand how my decision to simply detach from my body/mind and endure unwanted sexual encounters was connected to imprinting from my early childhood. I had let my self-worth be determined by other people's opinions and attitudes. In my need to be good, to not upset anyone, to be loved and accepted, I became reluctant to ever say no, a trait which definitely followed me into adulthood. I assumed that the unwelcome sexual interactions had been my fault somehow. Dovetailing with my reluctance to ever say no was a hymn I had sung hundreds of times in my younger years which had taken root in my subconscious: "Angry words oh let them never from my tongue unbridled slip. May the heart's best impulse ever, check them ere they soil the lip." I came to accept that it was a moral sin to even feel angry, let alone give voice to such thoughts or energy; and I suppressed any impulse to do so for a good many years.

Another example of a homily similarly drilled into my brain that I accepted as fact and which influenced my thinking and actions for much of my life was that money is the root of all evil. In fact, 1st Timothy 6:10 in the very King James version of the Bible I was given after my baptism actually reads: 'For the love of money is a root of all kinds of evil; which while some coveted after, they have erred from the faith, and pierced themselves through with many sorrows." That is a different lesson entirely. When I finally began examining the details of my first year of life, as well as reflecting on the unpredictability and insecurity, along with the psychological, verbal, and emotional abuse that occurred intermittently during the first two decades of my life, I became increasingly aware of fixed ideas, habits of mind and behaviors that seemed to stem from those seminal abuses I was exploring, a few of which have yet to completely vanish.

Surely there was something terribly wrong with me if the woman who gave birth to me didn't love me enough to take proper care of me, left me alone in my crib for hours at a time almost daily and then essentially abandoned me. I must have been inherently flawed, inferior in some fundamental way, unworthy and undeserving of love. I didn't just drive away my first mother but another mother and, initially at least, the next mother. I'm not good enough became a deeply engrained belief that shaped my personality and influenced my choices and conduct for years to come. I was constantly judging myself, trying to fix myself, edit myself, continually adapting my behavior in an effort to please others in order to gain their approval so they would love me. Very early in life, I developed the ability to read people. I could sense their moods, along with their emotional and mental states. This skill allowed me to adjust my actions to what the adults in control wanted from me. I became adept at deciphering the rules and following them, at deducing how people wanted me to behave so that I could act accordingly in order to please them and to avoid conflict or consequences. This ability also helped me maintain the image of being a good little girl. For much of my childhood and young adulthood I was constantly trying my best to be good enough, compliant enough, pretty enough, polite enough, quiet enough, and useful enough so that I would not be rejected or abandoned.

My study of drama and regular performances in theatrical productions

in high school and college had given me a boost in self-confidence. I am now conscious of the fact that the mask of acting became an acceptable and energizing form of being seen and heard. Inhabiting the personality and mannerisms of fictional or historic characters allowed me to come out in disguise, as it were. It gave me a safe place to shine while earning recognition and awards in the process. This cloaking device continued to serve me well throughout my undergraduate college years, during the three years I

spent earning a Master of Fine Arts degree in Acting, and through a summer at the American Conservatory Theater in San Francisco. It allowed me to enter the professional acting arena in the northern California Bay Area and eventually to touring for six months with a Shakespeare company playing the multifaceted character of Portia in *The Merchant of Venice*. Positive reviews boosted my confidence and helped me in beginning to rise

above (or possibly to bury more deeply in my unconscious) my low self-esteem issues and fear of rejection. The art of acting allowed me to present a polished persona to the world, while parts of my essential Self remained mostly hidden, unseen and unclaimed.

He was nineteen; I was eighteen when I fell in love with my first husband, a good looking, gentle, kindhearted, straight A student in the two-year college we were both attending on full scholarships (mine in theater and his academic). He was highly respected by teachers and students alike. I thought he was the closest thing to a saint I'd ever met. In retrospect, I think some part of my subconscious mind reasoned that if I was with him, my life would be perfect and that some of those saintly qualities would rub off on me. In reality, we were both naïve and inexperienced young people who came from completely different worlds and who barely knew each other when we married less than two years later. Our personalities had been formed from such divergent backgrounds and environments that, although we felt drawn to each other, and had declared our love and loyalty, it eventually became increasingly difficult to find common ground in terms of our individual needs and aspirations.

My new husband was like my father in some ways—intelligent, kind, stoical. And he too was often physically and emotionally absent. However, our histories differed radically. His parents had met on the Wind River Indian Reservation in Wyoming—home to the Eastern Shoshone and Northern Arapaho tribes—where his mother had been hired as a cook and his father as a mechanic. They began their life together in a two-room log cabin on a remote piece of land known as Owl Creek. Their first several children, including my husband, were born in that dirt-floored cabin before they moved into a small house in a nearby town that covered two square miles and had reached its highest population of not quite 4,000 people in 1960. My mother-in-law had birthed a dozen children, three of whom died in childbirth or shortly thereafter, in a span of twenty years. She was a true pioneer woman with remarkable survival skills. She raised chickens for their eggs and eventually for their food. She knew where to pick wild berries to turn into jam. I heard stories about her killing rattlesnakes and skinning deer and saw pictures of the shirts she hand-sewed for her nine children—the eight boys at least—out of flour sacks. My father-in-law worked long hours daily in his mechanic shop, and was a man of very few words. I, in contrast, had spent the bulk of my growing up years in the largest city in Kansas, with a population of over 250,000, an only child living in a three-bedroom house with an unpredictable stepmother who worked full time at various sales and secretarial jobs. When she was home, she seemed to never stop talking.

My husband and I moved to West Texas, a few months before the historically shocking event of President Kennedy's assassination on November 22, 1963, so that he could finish his double major undergraduate degree at a four-year Christian college. We lived briefly in one of the duplex barracks type buildings that had been converted into housing for married students before receiving a tip from a friend who was moving out of a very small apartment created from a single garage on the property of a widowed woman who lived in the house. The charge for rent was reduced in exchange for mowing the shared back lawn and doing a few other tasks now and then for the very generous and kind landlady. She never intruded on our space but we found ways to have short conversations with her by sharing cookies I'd baked and so on. I sensed that she was lonely and experiencing some medical challenges in her aging process.

We stayed three more years in Abilene so that my husband could complete a Bachelor of Divinity degree at the college. He managed to accomplish this while he was working at two part-time jobs: preaching every other Sunday at a church in a tiny, unincorporated cotton farming community a hundred miles away and working part-time as a gas station attendant.

One of the fringe benefits of the job had procured as a Secretary—thanks to those typing and shorthand classes I took while in Junior High School—to the Admissions and Placement Director of the college was free tuition for two classes each semester. This perk led to my taking drama classes, making friends in the Theater Department and appearing in several stage productions. I invited my new friends to our house to watch shows such as the Academy

Awards with me, and a few of us once travelled to Dallas together to see Peter, Paul and Mary in concert. These activities and friendships helped fill hours I would otherwise have spent by myself and helped decrease my loneliness.

When I became pregnant, we were a little surprised and a bit anxious, each in our own ways I think, yet happy. Learning that my job would be terminated as soon as I needed to wear maternity clothes—an unfortunate discrimination that wouldn't become illegal until more than a decade later—was disconcerting on several levels, particularly financially. My husband took on yet another part-time job to try to make ends meet.

A forward-thinking female professor I'd taken a class from who heard about me losing my job offered to pay me a very generous hourly fee to help her in her home. The work turned out to be several days of mostly polishing the large amount of silver she and her husband, also a professor who knew my husband as a student, owned. There seemed to be little else I could do to earn money at the time.

I went into labor on a Tuesday morning in June, nearly two months after the due date we were originally given by our doctor. In an effort to distract and comfort myself, I got out the Scrabble board my father and I had played on so many times, with his familiar handwriting on the score pad. I hadn't played the game in a good while since my husband had neither the time nor the inclination for that particular type of diversion. The unfolded board just fit on the two-person table in the tiny kitchen area of our living space. By sitting down on one side of the table, taking a turn, then switching to the other chair and taking a turn, all the while tracking the time between my contractions, I succeeded in getting through most of the day before needing to call the gas station where my husband was working to tell him I thought we should go to the hospital. Once there, I was quickly whisked away and—as was the custom in those days before expectant fathers were allowed into labor rooms—he was required to remain in the waiting room reserved for that purpose. A nurse appeared a few hours later to inform him that his daughter had been born.

Lying on my back under an incredibly bright light, legs spread-eagled, my feet in steel stirrups and experiencing particularly intense pain, I had encountered something I was never informed was going to occur. A mask came down over my face and a voice told me to count backwards from five. I only got to three. The next thing I knew, I was in a hospital bed with a nurse tapping me briskly on one cheek, saying, "Wake up, wake up! Don't you want to see your baby?" Another nurse appeared and placed a swaddled, puffy-cheeked infant with a full head of curly dark hair in my arms. I barely had time for my mind to register that this was the baby I had protected and nurtured inside my body for nine months before the nurse removed her from my arms and carried her out of the room. Watching the other nurse leave the room with a bloody sheet and, realizing it must be my blood, I wondered why I was bleeding. After two days of mostly sleeping, I was told I could get dressed to go home. Minutes later, the nurse brought my bundled baby into the room, deposited her on the bed saying I could dress her and, without further words, quickly exited. Completely alone with this miraculous, fragile person who was now totally dependent on me, I was petrified. Although I'd done a little "baby sitting" during my later high school years, I had never attempted to dress a real baby or even a small child in my life. We fashioned a bed for this new being now utterly dependent on our care in a pullout dresser drawer situated right next to my side of the double bed.

When our landlady died only a few weeks later, her son informed us she had stipulated that we move into the house and pay the same rent we had been paying, an incredibly generous gift on her part and at a much-needed time in our lives. We were able to rent out one of the two bedrooms of the house, which had its own entrance, to a friend, which also helped ease our financial situation.

A month or so later, sitting on a porch chair on a hot, dry summer day as evening approached, I was nursing my daughter while her father studied in the college library. As I gazed down at her face, marveling at the profound physical intimacy of feeding this miraculous human being who had emerged from my body, she opened her eyes and peered into mine Not quite letting go of my nipple completely, her little lips widened into a half smile. I knew in that instant that I would do my best to be the mother she deserved; I knew I would lay down my life for her.

After graduating with his straight A grade average still intact, my husband was soon offered ministerial jobs in three different locations in California. He chose the one in a university town in the greater Bay Area. Excelling at his job, my husband was deeply respected by everyone in the small congregation of less than a hundred members. Early each morning, he walked from the three-bedroom ranch style house we were given to live in, across an open field to his office in the church building, usually returning around dinner time. He took short breaks during the day at the basketball hoop at one edge of the church parking lot, sometimes joking that the hoop was the real reason he had said yes to that particular job offer. As soon as our daughter was old enough to walk across the field by herself, with me watching from one side and her dad from the other, nothing excited her more than carrying a bag lunch over to share with her Daddy. In the meantime, I played the part of minister's wife well, teaching Sunday School weekly and Vacation Bible School, serving as the church secretary, editing and typing a monthly newsletter, hosting dinners and special events in our home for the college students, and most Sundays, cooking and serving after-church services meals for various families in the congregation.

Our son's drug-free birth in California was radically different in nearly every way from giving birth four years earlier in Texas. My husband took notes during the Lamaze classes we attended together, accompanied me to most of my doctor's appointments and was with me from the beginning of my labor through our son's birth. He was there for me in a time when I desperately needed not to be alone and, for me, it was a pinnacle of intimacy in our relationship. Our new baby's almost four-year-old sister, convinced that she was his backup Mom, became his fierce protector from the beginning never once displaying any jealousy or indications of feeling displaced.

My husband and I were bound together by the vows we had taken and by our deep love for our children. Yet I was growing increasingly lonely in the marriage, craving a kind of emotional contact he didn't know how to offer and didn't seem to need himself.

Spending time with his children clearly brought him joy, though he often seemed to be happiest when he was in the library or by himself studying. In addition to his ministerial duties, he began auditing classes, including German, at the local University. When one of the friends I had made through the Drama Department at the college in Texas came to California looking for a place to stay, my husband immediately invited him to use our spare bedroom. Our guest often led singing during church services, our children liked him, and I was thrilled to have a familiar friend to talk with about things we had in common. During that time, my husband was spending two nights a week out of town in order to take an Ancient Hebrew Poetry and Covenant Theology in the Old Testament class with a favorite scholar/author of his at the Graduate Theological Union in Berkeley

The guilt I experienced after letting a comforting hug with a good friend—a virginal and still closeted gay man—lead to sex one night when my husband was away and my children sleeping, precipitated a soul-searing depression. My only thought was that I had failed utterly at being a good wife—much less a minister's wife—having now committed the grave sin of adultery. My feelings of remorse. and shame seemed more than I could bear.

I am standing in front of the medicine cabinet, holding a new razor blade I've taken out of a container. I wonder if I have to cut both my wrists. How do I do that? I have the thought that it will be too bloody. It will make too big a mess to clean up. I see a container in the medicine cabinet, a prescription medication for my husband's back pain. I fill the small cup by the sink with water and set it back down. I remove the cap from the container, and pour a bunch of the small white pills into my left hand. I set the container down on the edge of the sink. I throw the pills into my mouth, pick up the water and swallow all the tablets in one big gulp. I reach for the container to pour

**more pills into my hand but somehow knock
it over. The rest of the contents spill out into
the sink and onto the floor. The sound of the
pills falling and the sight is enough to push
a speck of light into the darkness—I cannot
do this to my children . . .**

I possess a hazy memory of my husband coming home with a young couple we had recently become acquainted with after they came to a church service. She must have taken our two children with her while her husband stayed at our house.

**I feel myself being held upright. I can't seem
to walk or talk. All I want is to sleep. They are
telling me that I have to keep walking. Saying
that if I can't stay awake they will have to take
me to the hospital.**

Some hours later, lying on the twin bed in the guest room, weeping silently, utterly bereft, I began trying to pray. There was absolutely no connection. It was as if a telephone line had been severed. There was simply nobody there. As I my tears continued, I had an inkling that the God of my beliefs did not exist. I now recognize that moment as the beginning of a long journey as a truth-seeker.

Not long after that pivotal event in my life, my husband arranged for us to move out of the minister's house into an apartment complex in town with a swimming pool, which we all enjoyed. I made friends with people who weren't church members and there were children nearby for ours to play with, something they had not had up to that point. My husband and I spent a little more time together, doing things that were very new for us, such as going to a movie once or twice. The one thing we never did was share our feelings, nor did we get the help we so clearly needed.

Perhaps we couldn't tell each other the truth because we were unable to clearly access our deeper feelings at that time or afraid to face them. Or, maybe we simply couldn't admit to or talk to each other about what we were actually feeling.

In hindsight, I think my husband then turned to the area of life that was most familiar, satisfying and comfortable for him—academic study. He decided to go back to school to work toward a doctorate degree. After being accepted and offered financial assistance at several prestigious graduate schools on both coasts, he chose University of California a Los Angeles.

In my mind I was assuming we would all go together, wherever his decision took us. I do not remember how we arrived at the decision to try a trial separation. I moved into a small, low-rent apartment in the town where we'd been living and subsequently applied for and was granted a scholarship to enroll in an Master of Fine Arts program in the theater department at the university there. He took our five-year-old daughter with him to southern California.

How did we come to agree to that arrangement? Did I just go along with his suggestion because I thought it was what he wanted? Did he think I would be happier? How could we have imagined it would possibly work to separate our family in that way and for the two of us to go to graduate school at the same time? Clearly, we were both unhappy, both feeling guilty, unable to communicate, flailing in the dark, and still terribly naive.

Less than a month later, I couldn't bear being away from my daughter, or the thought that she would feel I had abandoned her, nor did it feel right to keep my son separated from his father and sister. I repacked everything I'd just finished arranging, and drove to Los Angeles to reunite our family. My husband had been able to procure a space in the married students' apartments available at that time—old barracks made into small duplexes inside a large fenced area on Sepulveda Boulevard—although it seemed as if he was seldom there. He studied in the library on campus after his classes and often came home after the children and I were asleep.

At some point we made a decision to participate in an experimental shared living situation with a couple residing in the apartment just across from us—cooking and eating meals together, trading child care and so on. Although I enjoyed having an enthusiastic cooking partner and female friend, the trial was fairly short lived and did little if anything to improve my relationship with the father of my children. I don't think either of us could really articulate what we needed or wanted from each other at the time.

Securing an appointment for us at the UCLA counseling center gave me hope that professional advice might offer us a way forward. Near the end of our session, the therapist said he really couldn't help us, adding that we were like two people standing at either end of a swimming pool and neither of us was willing to jump in. He ended the session saying, "I don't know how I can help you."

What if we'd been able to be seen by a more skilled therapist who could have suggested something, offered us some kind of help or activities that might have at least given us hope? Could that have changed the ultimate outcome?

My husband moved out of our duplex apartment physically a short time later, into a house with a few other graduate students and within walking distance of the university so that I would have a car. Finding myself essentially a single mom with two young children and very little money, I was sometimes able to sell my government-issued food stamps in order to pay for other necessities, such as the special shoes I was told my son needed to prevent his feet from pronating. Having heard from someone that grocery stores were forced to discard good food that hadn't been sold after a certain number of days, I tried dumpster diving late at night while my children were both asleep in the car. Though I did find things like potatoes, cabbage, and carrots that were still perfectly fine for cooking and eating, the surreptitious nature of the activity and the feeling that I was doing something illegal prevented me from continuing that particular practice for very long.

At the end of that summer, I went back to northern California with both children, secured subsidized housing for us, and we all three began school that fall: nursery, elementary, and graduate. Still holding onto the thought that my husband and I would somehow find a way to repair and improve our relationship and that our family would be together again, I couldn't bring myself to think about divorce. He finally initiated the action nearly two years later. We had no assets and had already divided our belongings so the procedure was simple. In spite of the fact that it clearly needed to be done, and we had both moved on to other relationships, signing the divorce papers was heart-wrenching and one of the saddest days of my life. I remember calling my father and step-mother crying. My father said "Well honey, life's not a bowl of cherries," and she said "Have you got a good lawyer?" Neither response was the least bit helpful or what I needed to hear in that moment. I knew my husband and I still loved each other. I felt as if I'd failed in some fundamental way. Perhaps he felt something similar. He sent me what little money he could each month and our children spent summers with him, as well as long weekends when they became old enough to fly alone.

While working toward my Master of Fine Arts degree, teaching undergraduate acting classes and dramatizing patient roles for third-year medical students to help pay my rent and other bills, I met the man who would eventually become my second husband when we were cast opposite each other in a theatrical production.

After my first marriage ended, I was reluctant to commit to monogamy in a sexual relationship again. Having broken my marriage vows and still feeling guilty about it, I thought it better to avoid such a promise. I had difficulty trusting others, especially anyone I began a romantic relationship with, not to leave me. I hadn't yet understood that I needed to be able to love myself instead of depending on someone else to generate my self-worth. I was afraid to trust love. I had no confidence that any relationship would last and an underlying fear of future abandonment. I came to realize eventually that, subconsciously at least, I must have needed to have someone in the wings, so to speak, an extra relationship to fall back on so I wouldn't be left alone. I am aware that there was also some rebellion at play in the decisions I was making at that time, stemming from my resistance to being pressured to think and act in a way that someone else felt I should. Layered into my reluctance to commit to a monogamous relationship was the fact that I had never had the chance to explore my own sexuality before I married. Giving myself permission to do that led to some surreptitious and ill-advised decisions on my part, yet it also helped me reach a point of being able, ultimately, to freely choose and commit to a life-long monogamous relationship.

Paradoxically, I began to notice how deeply habituated I was to continually adapting and simply going along with what others seemed to want rather than making any effort to communicate what I might want or how I actually felt about something. I gradually became more conscious of the fact that I always let the other person in a relationship define situations and make decisions for me in order to avoid their potential upset, displeasure or rejection. I eventually became aware of how often I felt irritated, or resentful underneath my show of acquiescence. Occasionally, I can still catch myself slipping into a tuning out and disconnecting response any time I begin to feel judged or sense that I am, even on a subtle level, being made wrong. I notice that I immediately feel vulnerable and experience an energetic impulse to hide or protect myself. And, I sometimes still mistake someone's impassioned opinion about a matter as disparagement or as a critical response to something I've said or done. I'm able to recognize when that is happening and to change my response, at least most of the time, yet the habit is deeply ingrained. I am no longer seeking approval from others yet I do catch myself sometimes still hoping for that.

My Jewish husband, the product of a dialectical culture that thrives on passionate discourse, was raised to express his feelings fully and completely as they surfaced, including what might be called healthy anger. It was a trait I was so unaccustomed to that, while some small part of me almost admired this ability, I felt easily overpowered by the intensity of his efforts to engage me in this particular way. Early in our relationship, long before we married, he encouraged, even pushed me, to express my thoughts and feelings, whatever they were. Years later he confessed to starting arguments with me in order to "draw out your energy." What he perceived as healthy exchanges

I took as escalating criticism; and I experienced the energy being directed at me as if I were being physically and emotionally pummeled. When this occurred, I would retreat, simply disappear for hours, or sometimes decide that the relationship was over.

There came a day when I did express myself and my husband and I soon became engaged in what seemed to me to be an escalating argument as he became more animated and his voice got louder. I became so angry that I found a seldom used tube of red lipstick and used it to quickly write a message to him on a wall-to-wall mirror over the two-sink counter in our bathroom. I wrote some awful things, in my estimation, using several swear words I had never uttered aloud, before grabbing my car keys, slamming the front door behind me as hard as I could and driving to a movie theater.

I have no clue what film may have been playing in that theater; however, halfway through the movie, I went into great angst. Ruminating about what I'd done, I felt I'd surely ruined my relationship with my husband, and that he would never forgive me. Daring to hope there was some chance he hadn't yet seen the missive I'd scrawled across the bathroom mirror I left the theater immediately and drove home. Creeping quietly and slowly through the front door, feeling small, childish, and dejected, with tears in my eyes, I was stunned when my husband greeted me with open arms. He grabbed me gently by my shoulders, looked me in the eyes and said enthusiastically, "Dawn, do you realize that this is the first time you've gotten in touch with your anger in the moment you were feeling it, and were able to express that!?" I later read somewhere that those who feel unloved in childhood almost never feel comfortable expressing anger, or even disappointment, especially with someone they love.

Over the years, I gradually become more willing to communicate my own point of view without feeling guilty or ashamed. My husband and I began using communication skills that supported us in having productive discussions instead of arguments when disagreements arise, and I learned to set limits on the amount of time I am able to engage in such exchanges. We came up with a strategy many years ago that has proven practical and beneficial. When a conflict between us begins to escalate and we feel ourselves becoming more deeply entrenched in our personal positions on some matter, either of us can retrieve a tattered white rag on a stick which we keep in a special place, and wave it in the air. This action does not mean the person waving it surrenders to the other's position. It is simply a reminder that we have agreed to never make a personal point of view or preference more important than our commitment to our relationship. Another strategy we began using when we disagree about a practical decision that needs to be made is to each say how important our preference is by choosing a number between one and ten. We agreed to be honest about the number and to go with what whatever number is higher. We have been pleasantly surprised at how well this has worked 99% of the time and how much wasted energy it has saved in extended discussions or arguments. We passed this white flag, which we originally found in my father-in-law's house after his death, on to our youngest daughter and her partner when they married. We rarely find a need to wave the "peace flag" any more though if we do, any piece of white material seems to suffice.

According to the International Society for Traumatic Stress Studies (https://istss.org/home) and other sources, the effects of early childhood abuse can have significant repercussions in adulthood—emotionally, mentally, and even physically. And yet, all trauma also provides an opportunity for growth and transformation. There are definitely times when I still struggle to identify and articulate my authentic feelings. I occasionally experience short bouts of depression or sadness when my mind perceives that I have been misunderstood or that I am being judged, or criticized for the way I think or feel. I notice myself caught between becoming upset about not being seen and simply burying my feelings. My brain still reacts when I'm told I *should* do something, and I continue to find escalating volume in spirited discussions that sometimes turn into arguments energetically draining. However, I'm now usually able to express what I am feeling when I am feeling it, or sometimes after some private reflection. I no longer *believe* everything I think or identify with every emotion that arises. I have come to recognize, and focus on, the positive things—such as empathy, resourcefulness and adaptability—that have come to me in life in spite of, or possibly even engendered by the distress and trauma I experienced before my birth, in my infancy and during my childhood. I have also learned not only that demons can turn out to be angels in disguise but that what seems like adversity can turn into grace.

Section Three

Pathways to Healing

Nine

Portals to Awakening

Three days' ardent yearning is enough to obtain Divine grace.
~ Sayings of Sri Ramakrishna

*A perception, sudden as blinking, that subject and object are one, will
lead to a deeply mysterious, wordless understanding: and by this
understanding you will awaken to the truth.*

~ Hung Po

In 1978, a longtime friend told me about a residential meditation
retreat she had recently attended. She said it was the most powerful
practice she'd ever experienced. She also mentioned that while she
was participating in this three-day meditative practice, she reached
a place where she faced death. That sounded a bit scary, so I didn't
think much more about it as I continued working on my massage
school certification training and exploring various yogic and
meditative practices.

Close to two years later, I ended up taking part in the type of
retreat my friend had spoken of, which was called a Self-Realization or
Enlightenment Intensive. A bodyworker friend had introduced me to
the person who was organizing what she referred to as an "Advanced
Intensive" being put together for people already familiar with this
type of retreat. In fact, a majority of the people in attendance had
been participating in or leading these three-day residential retreats
for a decade or more. Since I was going be a "newcomer" to this
particular meditative approach, I was asked to complete a questionnaire
about other types of growth work I had done before being invited
to join what would soon become known as The Annual California
Enlightenment Intensive. I went with a mutual friend who had also
filled out a questionnaire and been invited to attend. We were both

a bit nervous about the whole endeavor. As we were having a light dinner in a cafe before driving to our destination, The Headlands Institute in Sausalito, we agreed that if either one of us decided we wanted to leave at any time, we'd give each other a sign and simply get up and go out together. Instead, we discovered something that would change both our lives in significant ways.

Upon our arrival, the night before the formal beginning of the three days, we noticed that most of the people gathering seemed to know each other well; there was a lot of hugging and talking going on. We were welcomed by the organizer, shown where we'd be sleeping in the dormitory style set-up, and each chose a bed. We had signed our names to a sheet of paper we'd each been given, agreeing to go by a few rules that would be in place during the three-days. These guidelines included following the schedule, using only the technique being taught, eating only the food we were given, setting aside sexual activity, smoking, drinking, recreational drugs, gossiping and so on.

There was an orientation type talk that evening in which the staff—leaders, assistants and cooks—were introduced and we were given information about the rather daunting schedule, which would run from 6:00 a.m. to 11:30 p.m. for the next two days. The last day would end several hours earlier. A short talk that included words of reassurance, support and inspiration was given before those who were already practiced in this type of retreat were told to choose their question and take it to bed with them. Anyone taking their first Intensive was instructed to use the question "Who am I?" Old-timers were reminded to choose between Who, What, Another or Life. Still a bit nervous about the uncertainty of what might or might not occur in the next three days, it took me a while to get to sleep. We were awakened the next morning by a hand-held bell rung three times and the instruction to be in the main room ready for an introductory talk in fifteen minutes. A few people looked sleep deprived and slightly uneasy while others were all smiles, seemingly eager to begin.

The schedule for the first and second days of the retreat included twelve approximately forty-minute dyads. We were instructed to pair up with a different partner each time. There were other activities on the schedule such as walking contemplation, working contemplation, silent contemplation, and a longer talk from one of the three experienced individuals who were co- leading that particular retreat. There was a rest period as well as three meals and an afternoon snack each day. The major activity, however, was clearly the dyads.

I found this partner assisted communication a refreshing and energizing format. It seemed superior to meditating alone, reciting a mantra, focusing on an object or even concentrating solely on my breath. The practice was to sit down opposite any other participant. On my turn to receive my instruction, "Tell me who you are," I was to put my attention on what was most real about who I am, in that moment, to intend to experience that directly, and to be open. I would then communicate to my partner whatever had come up for me. I was listened to without interruption, or any comment beyond "Thank you" when a resonant gong rang indicating it was time to give our partners their questions and to receive whatever they had to communicate. The roles were reversed every five minutes during each forty-minute dyad. This distinct way of listening was, in and of itself, an extremely useful exercise, well worth cultivating; and it was a noticeable contrast to the so often hurried and incomplete communications with others in public places, or even with family members, which are sometimes carried on while multi-tasking or without full receptive attention.

I was particularly impressed by the fact that the process being taught empowers the individual, rather than the leaders. I was greatly relieved that it didn't seem to be connected to any particular religion or belief system, and that we were not asked to join a center, a sect, or a movement at the end of the three days. At the time, I didn't fully understand the subtleties of the specific contemplative technique we were using. However, I did notice that when I put my attention on myself, intending to experience, and being open to who I am before reporting what occurred, my communications eventually grew simpler and a bit more concise. I also observed that I had some deep attachments to certain ways of thinking about myself. Close to the end of the three days, I became consciously aware that I was the one asking "Who am I?"

My main takeaway from that first three-day retreat—in addition to the gift of being relieved of a multitude of daily tasks and having delicious food cooked by someone else served to me three times a day—was the power of the primary activity, basically combining an age-old Rinzai Zen koan practice with a modern communication technique. I was affected by the depth of the contact that grew between my partners and myself as the dyads continued. I noticed that the deep listening galvanized my attention and that it opened my mind and heart. It made me think of the uniquely wise and gentle Fred Rogers, on his long running television show *Mr. Rogers' Neighborhood,* when he would remind both the children and the adults watching that "the best thing we can do for each other is to listen with our ears and our hearts." In the years to come it also brought to mind Thich Nhat Hanh's concept of compassionate listening, which he defined as the kind of listening that can relieve suffering, listening that helps us keep compassion alive while we give another a chance to "speak out and suffer less."

Being listened to without being interrupted , contradicted, or corrected was something I seldom experienced during my childhood except when I was with my grand-parents. As a result, over the years, I had developed a habitual unconscious pattern of suppressing my deeper thoughts and emotions, and of not expecting to be closely listened to. Although I did not experience any major transformational breakthrough during that initial three-day retreat, I felt more open in a new way. I was energized and activated by the activity and I knew that I wanted to go deeper. I left feeling grateful for the structure, the precision of the schedule, the simple, nourishing, mindfully prepared food, and the attentive, caring staff. It was the most potent and promising tool for growth I had ever encountered.

In the months that followed, I participated in a number of these unique on-site meditative retreats. I learned that they were held in different settings—from various types of large retreat centers to private homes—and that the number of participants could vary from dozens of people to only eight or ten individuals along with a small staff. The second or third Intensive I attended was held in a small treehouse located on a lush and magical forested property in central

California. I believe there were ten participants. We all climbed up some kind of rigged ladder to emerge in the middle of this circular structure for our dyads. At night, we slept on the floor right next to each other with our feet facing the center opening. I had learned that the word master was used to refer to the person leading these types of retreats. In this particular context, being the master refers to a person who has the experience, knowledge, and skill to teach the technique being used. The role also requires an ability to stay focused, present and available to participants, supporting them through anything that arises which might deter their contemplation or progress, and to hold the space.

The Treehouse Intensive, as we later referred to it, was co-mastered by two good friends who had led many of these three-day, or occasionally longer, residential retreats for a number of years, including organizing and leading one per month for a period of time. During that particular retreat, I was receiving the instruction "Tell me who you are" from each dyad partner. Around the middle of the second day, it became clear to me that there was one participant in the small group whom I was avoiding, though I didn't really know why. I decided to confront whatever was making me hesitant, and at the beginning of the next dyad, I sat down opposite that particular other. Halfway through our dyad, my physical body seemed to expand beyond any discernible form, and then disappear entirely. At the same time, my mind went completely blank. It seemed as if I somehow merged with the being sitting opposite me. There was simply no discernible perception of any distinction between the two of us, or of us being in any way different or separate, at some core level of reality. Whatever I was and whatever that individual was, it was the same, and it had nothing to do with our personalities, our gender or our physical bodies. In the midst of this recognition, I gradually became aware of existing both inside and outside of my physical form. Quite unexpectedly, some unique phenomenon arose in the form of seeing ribbons of bright, golden-tinged light coming out of the top of my head and joining with the same light coming out of my partner's head. Time and space and words ceased to exist. I was truly speechless.

I don't remember if I was the listening or the contemplating partner when this occurred, nor do I remember what my partner might have been experiencing during that time. It took me awhile to realize we had come to the end of the dyad and to finally manage to say "thank you" to that individual. I think there was a break right after that when we all climbed down from the treehouse. I almost felt as if I was learning how to move inside some new thing called a body. I asked to speak with one of the masters. We sat down in the grass below the treehouse and I finally regained my ability to speak, reporting as best I could what had occurred. I felt deeply contacted, seen, and heard as I expressed my certainty in regard to this timeless, wordless, inexplicable experience. I was then instructed to change the question I was contemplating to "What am I?" an inquiry I have continued to use, and which has continued to deepen over the years to this day. That remarkably powerful new awareness fundamentally changed my relationship with others. It was as if I'd been wearing sunglasses that had been suddenly removed. I began seeing other people in a completely new and different way. I perceived a sameness between myself and all others at an intrinsic level that was not in any way connected to that person's physical appearance, gender, personality, background, beliefs, ideas, or disposition. I began to want to treat people better after that—not from some teaching that said I should, but from what I had actually experienced.

Less than a year later, I completed a rigorous, ten-day training course to learn how to lead Enlightenment Intensives. The first instruction I received during the critiques when I was assigned to be a monitor on one of the practice Mini-Intensive , was to come more from myself, to be willing to be seen, rather than tiptoeing around the edges as if I were trying to be invisible. After my first turn in being the master, and giving my self-evaluation, the feedback from the observing instructor was " don't be so hard on yourself; stop trying so hard to be good." Sitting in a dyad during one of my fellow students' practice Intensives, something occurred that caught me by surprise. The only word I could come up with to describe it was innocence, an awareness that I was innocent. It was as if a ray of sunshine had landed on and in me, briefly. I didn't consciously connect it at that time with my birth mother's rejection of me or the fact that her actions had nothing to do with me. I just noticed that I felt a little less restricted in some way; there was a small shift in my belief that I was never going to be "good enough." By the end of that course, I knew I had met a teacher, not in the sense of some sort of guru or elevated being, but a person with integrity and wisdom who would mentor me in developing my ability to share this particular methodology which I intuitively sensed would lead me to reclaiming some essential part of myself that I had lost.

The following year, I was invited to come back as an assistant on the same course and my husband completed the training. He then gave an inspiring three-day Intensive with the passion and skill of a natural born teacher and with certainty born of his own experience with the technique being taught, before then becoming a crucial and dependable assistant for me as I continued organizing and leading such events.

During that same time period, I was a participant in a two-week Intensive held in our home, mastered by the person I had trained with to give Intensives. In my contemplation, I soon came face-to-face with personality traits in myself that I hadn't been consciously aware of—my criticalness, my hypocrisy, my need to be in control, my obsessive concerns about the environment, and so on. In the daily lectures, we were urged to be open and to be willing to go forward beyond the predictable, beyond what we were already conscious of. We were reminded that many states will come and go and to keep doing our best. I continued facing my ego attachments and fixations, such as wanting my life to look good, noticing my constant yearning to be seen as a good parent, a good mate, a good person.

By the beginning of the second week, my inner critic seemed unstoppable. I had fallen into abject sorrow and unrelenting self judgements I could hardly bear as I re-experienced the deep regret, and remorse I was still carrying regarding the failure of my first marriage. I recognized how completely unconscious and unprepared I had been when I married at age nineteen. I naively believed that getting married meant I'd always be happy, be taken care of, be cherished. I assumed my husband would become my best friend and my ally in life. The reality of my physical and emotional loneliness in the relationship had felt like abandonment. At the time, however, I didn't believe my feelings were valid. I was certain that it meant I wasn't giving enough or I wanted too much or I expected too much. Even when both of us stepped outside our relationship into intimate encounters with other people, I was convinced it only happened because there was something lacking in me. If I had been a better person—more patient, more mature, had fewer expectations—then everything would surely have worked out.

As I struggled to continue following the instruction to communicate whatever was coming up for me as a result of my contemplation, and to be open, willing to step into the unknown, I was confronted with a pounding headache unlike anything I'd ever encountered. It felt as if needles were being pushed into my eyeballs against my will. As evening approached, I began feeling nauseated as well. Simply sitting upright was difficult, and staying in contact with my dyad partners seemed close to impossible. I felt ashamed, weak, ugly, and as if I was being tortured. This physical state continued through most of the following day until it vanished as mysteriously as it had begun without the aid of any drug or therapeutic intervention.

Pushing through pain, fears, tears, distractions, energy fluctuations, and my habitually self-critical mind, I persisted with the practice, one day at a time. During the last one-hour walking contemplation period, I was moving slowly along the sidewalk on a nearby block, noticing trees, grasses, flowering plants, the sky, the clouds, even the houses I was passing as if I was seeing them for the first time. They appeared more defined, more colorful, more vibrant than usual somehow. The air smelled fresh and clean as if it had just rained. At some point I became aware of a baby wailing inside a nearby house as though it was in distress, and that stopped me in my tracks. It seemed as if I was that baby. Was that how I had sounded to the neighbors whose reports finally led to the police breaking into my birth mother's apartment and to my being rescued?

As the crying continued, my mind shifted and I began thinking about a very conscious decision I had made, before remarrying, not to have another child. After a protracted effort to persuade me to change my mind, my now husband had eventually accepted my decision. A stream of words abruptly broke through my thoughts, appearing like large letters on a chalkboard in my brain: "To be free you must be willing to be wrong about everything." The words kept appearing over and over until it seemed as if my head would explode. At that moment I let go of my preconceived ideas, my self-judgements, my preferences, my certainty. I just laid that burden down and metaphorically fell to my knees in the middle of that uneven, sun-dappled sidewalk with little shoots of green grass growing up through the cracks, and surrendered everything I thought I knew.

The first enlightenment intensive I had attended became an annual event held in various retreats centers in northern California. I continued to take part in this large Annual Intensive, either as a participant, a chief monitor, a senior monitor, or as the leader. One year, as a participant, sitting opposite my partner during one of the last dyads of the three days, something extraordinary transpired. The light in the room began to change perceptibly. It became brighter, yet softer—a golden, warm, protective glowing light—and I sensed my deceased father's presence. Simultaneously dozens of luminous beings seemed to fill the large, barn-like space we were in. I saw them clearly in my inner vision; I could feel the purity of their nature. They were everywhere. There was nowhere they were not. It was as if some invisible veil had lifted, allowing me to experience something that had been there all along. Struggling to communicate to my dyad partner what was happening, I was flooded with emotion, along with the realization that nobody had ever not wanted me to experience the love that was flooding the room at that moment, and that love was also inside me. I had never completely opened to the undeniable reality that was penetrating my being, which was that I had never truly been alone. I had never not been who and what I am. I simply didn't have that truth mirrored to me during a crucial time in my life when the absence of the consistent, responsive and loving relationship I deserved was a serious threat to my neurological and cognitive development.

That experience was life-altering for me. It was another small step in setting me on a path toward liberating myself from the effects of my birth mother's abusive neglect and failure to claim me, and from the subsequent confusion and uncertainty I experienced so often during my early childhood. It began to erode the deep-seated beliefs buried in my subconscious that I would never be enough, that I was inherently flawed somehow and that I didn't deserve to be truly loved because the woman who brought me into this world had neglected and then rejected me. I couldn't really live from that idea anymore. I still had vestiges of it, and a number of years would pass before those would dissolve completely, yet that false belief was no longer as deeply fixed in my being.

In the fall of 1983, I was filling the position of senior monitor for the Fifth Annual California Enlightenment Intensive for an individual who had been leading these types of Intensives for many years in a variety of venues. This particular one was being held at a spa-like mineral hot springs located on a large nature preserve in northern California. There were around thirty of us gathered in the attic room of the one hotel-like building that existed there at that time. The room had no electricity so we were ringing the bells that signaled changeovers at the end of each dyad by hand instead of playing them on a cassette tape. The space was lit with lanterns after dark, giving the wooden walls that surrounded us a kind of glow. During the first dyad at 6:15 on the second morning, a participant cried out, "**I just want everybody to wake up!**" Apparently, at least one guest, sleeping in the lower part of the building, WAS awakened from his sleep, albeit not in the way the participant was referring to, by what he heard, and he very quickly complained to the front desk. Hearing the manager's angry footsteps on the stairway as he stomped up the stairs towards our attic refuge, I instinctively moved to intercept him like a lioness defending her cubs. Opening the door, I received his upset, told him I understood what he was saying, and that the person leading our retreat would come down to speak with him shortly. As he somewhat reluctantly turned and descended the stairs, I quickly began considering ways in which we might set the group up outside if necessary. As I reflect on it now, I'm aware that my brief discussion with the manager that morning was a pivotal moment for me in reclaiming the power of simply being me and being willing to be seen as my Self. When I later asked the individual mastering that particular Intensive what he'd said to the manager, he replied "Oh I just contacted him." I was in awe of his answer at the time and yet looking back on it now, I realize that was exactly what I had also done. When the participants set up for the next Dyad, in another masterful action, this wise leader said nothing about what had occurred, simply instructing everyone to continue getting across to their partners whatever was coming up for them as a result of their contemplation.

During a slightly different type of five-day meditative retreat with a group of people who had taken a number of Intensives, while I was sweeping the floors during a working contemplation period, I was suddenly struck with an unadulterated and absolute revelation. No matter where my eyes landed—whether on another individual, a pair of shoes, a tree outside the window—absolutely everything I could see or touch had the same ineffable energy or quality. In that moment, I wanted nothing more than to bow to every person and to every object I laid eyes on. Cleaning the floor and lining up the shoes by the door did not seem like a task that needed to be completed. It was simply a natural action of pure joy in serving others. I found myself in a blessedly blissful bubble for the rest of that day. The following day, however, I was plunged into an opposite state of being as all my mental baggage began to intrude. Struck by how out of touch I was, in my normal life, with the actuality I'd just experienced, I felt in that moment that the effort to live my life in harmony with the truth I had encountered was like trying to move forward while buried up to my neck in mud. My failure to consistently treat others as what they actually are seemed to me the equivalent of constantly spitting in the face of God, and I quickly fell into deep and utter despair. I communicated this in private to the person leading the retreat, who listened compassionately before reminding me that the truth itself doesn't change or go away. "You might forget about it or bury it in the mud, yet it is always there."

Maybe if we have hidden ourselves from others long enough, we get stuck in the muck of our own making it more difficult to let go of our armor and let ourselves be seen as who we actually are. Maybe we get so used to identifying with the clouds we actually forget that the sun is always there.

My understanding of the dyad meditation technique I was practicing and teaching gradually increased. I came to appreciate more and more the power found in the reciprocal gift of being fully present for another, open to and simply listening to that individual without interior monologue or judgements about what is being said, and in turn being received and heard in the same receptive, non-judgmental way. I began to understand that it is okay to feel however I feel, to grasp the fact that thoughts are simply thoughts, emotions are just emotions, and both are continually changing, much like the clouds or the weather. The only power our thoughts have is the power we give them. Eventually I was able, at least some of the time, to observe the internal chatter of my wandering and easily distracted mind, as I might view the constantly moving canopy in our atmosphere, without evaluating, denying, or believing every thought that arises. I am continuing to grow in my ability to open to whatever appears with less self-condemnation, evaluating, labeling, and ego attachment. I am more able to discriminate between an individual and that person's point of view or preferences. The more I experienced the efficacy of the process as I practiced it myself, the more confident I became in my ability to teach it to others.

In the mid 1980s, while we were visiting various temples and friends in Japan, my husband and I were offered a private audience with the head priest of a Jodo Shin Shu (Pure Land School) Buddhist temple in Kamakura. Before meeting this individual, I had conjured up an image in my mind that led me to think we would likely enter a sparsely furnished room with a gray-bearded, wizened man sitting cross legged on a pillow, who might ask us a few questions without answers before dismissing us. Instead, we were ushered into a small room with a large and quite cluttered wooden desk taking up at least half the space. The person behind the desk, wearing thick, black-rimmed glasses, rose to greet us, smiling as if we were old friends, and motioned for us to sit on the two chairs set up on the opposite side of his desk. He rang a small bell and almost immediately a tray of tea and small cakes arrived, delivered by a robed monk who set the platter down carefully in front of us. He then backed out of the room while bowing to our host.

Despite his high status in that community, Fukiyoshi Sensei could not have been more open and gracious, welcoming us amicably, as if he had nothing more pressing or important to do. Fully present and attentive in his contact, he seemed to take a great deal of delight in telling us stories, speaking in a blend of English and Japanese, and chuckling often. When my husband shared a little bit about what we had been experiencing from our participation in the meditative retreats called Enlightenment Intensives back in the United States, the Sensei smiled sweetly at us and then casually said something profound: "Oh yes, yes, such realizations are good, very nice, but the important thing is how they affect one's behavior in life. Do they help you treat others better?" Years later, remembering his remark. I'm reminded of a quote by the current Dalai Lama: "My religion is kindness."

Our seven-month-old daughter, who had been sitting quietly and wide-eyed in my lap, had not taken her eyes off our host. As he fixed his attention on her, my husband remarked that she already seemed to have a strong ego. Sensei made a comment about her innocence before commenting that, "as our egos develop, we start becoming critical and making judgments, but a strong sense of self is important in order to one day surrender to the Formless One." I have recalled our encounter with this great soul, and pondered his words, many times over the years.

Though I had never consciously taken any vow to do so, and I certainly blundered a few times along the way, I was able to bond with and care for my two older children in a way that my birth mother had simply been unable to do with me. When I was blessed with a third child, who was sitting on my lap in the Sensei's small office that day, after two miscarriages on the way to meeting her, I felt I had been given a chance to parent in a more conscious way, and to more deeply appreciate the gift of motherhood. My older daughter would later say in an interview that she felt she and her brother were mothered with the same love and attention I was giving to her younger sister, but that I was experiencing being a mother differently due to a change inside me.

Enlightenment, when used in a spiritual context, may be referred to as Awakening, Bodhi, Samadhi, Pure Awareness, Satori, Kensho, or simply seeing one's true nature. In general, the terminology references direct, conscious contact with something that is outside of physical and emotional realms, beyond the senses, beyond our personalities, and beyond the workings of the mind. It occurs when dualities disappear and the boundaries between the one who is experiencing and the experience itself dissolve. Eckhart Tolle notes that awakening could be defined as a shift out of the egoic state or as a shift of consciousness into the state of presence that will change how we experience our life as well as our relationships with others. For some individuals this may occur as a seemingly random and unexpected seismic change in consciousness, or as a quantum leap from one level of awareness to another. For others, it may be a gradual unfolding over time, perhaps over a lifetime. An old friend with decades of experience in various spiritual traditions says in his deceptively simple yet wise and inspirational booklet, *Connecting with Eternity,* that "Enlightenment is not something you get; it's something you relax into." I once heard the American Buddhist author Robert Thurman suggest, in a talk he was giving, that enlightenment is where you are asleep and awake at the same time, there is no duality. Regardless of what name we may give to it, Awakening is not the end result of some arduous journey that leads to perfection or to everlasting serenity, nor is it the end of adversity, or of life challenges. We still inhabit human bodies; we still have thoughts, feelings, opinions, expectations, preferences, and personalities.

As the well-known actor/narrator and Buddhist priest Peter Coyote mentions in his latest book, *Zen in the Vernacular,* such experiences can alter "our worldview profoundly alerting us to connections and relationships with everything from a different perspective." Jack Kornfield reminds us in his book, *After the Ecstasy, the Laundry,* that whatever new levels of awareness or realizations we may experience, we are still faced with our day-to-day tasks, whatever those may be.

In many ways, our experiences of waking up to the reality of our connection to all beings and all things is the beginning of a journey rather than the end of one. We have ample opportunities to notice our thoughts and emotions as they occur without getting quite as attached to or identified with them, to stop believing everything we think, to pause before saying everything we think, and so on. Living life as the embodied beings that we are continues to teach us. Parenting is a spiritual practice; marriage is a spiritual practice; surviving a life-threatening illness is a spiritual practice; aging is a spiritual practice; staying present in the now and in the face of whatever arises in our lives or in our environment is a spiritual practice. Truly, there is not one moment that is not an opportunity for shifts in consciousness, for deeper awareness, for Awakening, for letting our true selves arise.

While sitting in front of my computer, I try to remember to pause every so often, let my fingers rest, and take a few deep breaths as I gaze out the second-story window to the right of my desk. I often marvel at the constant change and movement—by the moment, by the hour, by the day, by the season—as far as my eyes can see. I can't resist smiling at the sassy squirrels scampering across the rooftop or playing tag in the trees and along fence-tops, or the chickadees somersaulting through the air in the spring. I fall into awe every autumn as the leaves change color and float gracefully to the ground or travel down the street catching a ride on a gentle breeze. Sometimes

I am enveloped by an exquisite and unique silence and a vastness I seem to merge with. Once in a while I stare in wonder at the sight of a full moon slowly rising above the treetops. Time ceases to exist and I am graced with an experience of union and peace that is truly beyond understanding.

> The moon's the same old moon,
> The flowers exactly as they were,
> Yet I've become the thingness
> Of all the things I see!
> ~ Shidō Bu'nan

Ten

Lessons from the Elderly, the Ill, and the Dying

Empathetic precision is about being aware of the whole context of how a person is hurting…attuning ourselves to what matters most to this person in this particular moment.

~ Frank Ostaseski

When you feel yourself to be a vehicle of kindness, an instrument of love, there is more to the deed than the doer and what's been done; you yourself feel transformed.

~ Stephen Levine

After suffering two miscarriages in my early forties my husband and I were deeply grateful to help usher a new being into this world during my forty-third year of life. Already teaching English and Humanities full time, he took on a second job teaching classes at a community college at night so that I could work full time as a stay-at-home mom. It was a role and a responsibility that I found immensely satisfying as well as enormously exhausting at times.

After about a year and a half, my husband noted that my contributions to our conversations at the end of his work day were becoming a bit—as he put it—limited. We began talking about ways that I might be able to exercise other parts of my brain by doing something new and creative just for myself. This conversation led to my enrolling in a nearby graduate school where I intended to work slowly toward a degree in Counseling Psychology. As often happens in life, I was led in a different direction. A newly designed certification program entitled "Awakening to Life and Death" caught my attention, in large part because my father had recently been diagnosed with inoperable, metastasized lung cancer.

A component in completing that particular program was an internship that required spending time on a weekly basis with at least one individual nearing death. I accomplished this by becoming a hospice volunteer, which allowed me to adapt my massage therapy and listening skills to being with individuals approaching the end of their lives.

I was both energized and a bit nervous after receiving my first assignment as a volunteer. Having called to confirm the day and time of my visit, and arriving at the address I'd been given, I sat in my car for a few minutes to quiet my mind by focusing on my breath. I remember saying spontaneously, out loud, "Please help me keep my mouth shut and my heart open" before getting out of my car. The freshly mown grass on either side of the walkway to the front door was bordered by neatly trimmed flowering hedges. When I knocked gently on a door that was ever so slightly ajar, a voice called out to me to come in. I noticed my name listed on a schedule for the day taped on the wall just inside the door. It looked as if various relatives or friends had signed up every few hours during the day, to make sure their loved one and friend was never left alone for long. I could see a hospital bed in a nearby room and I followed the sound of the weak yet friendly voice.

The room I entered was not a master bedroom but a smaller space that had been lovingly arranged for the comfort of the woman in the hospital bed. The space was quiet, clean and free of clutter, with necessities in their place on a bedside table. There was a beautiful bouquet of fresh flowers on another small table, and just enough other furniture to make the area feel welcoming.

Eileen told me she was tired but not in pain. She then said, smiling, "I have done all I can." We spoke very little. As I massaged her feet slowly and gently, she began to relax her entire body. I then moved to her bedside, sitting on the chair provided there, holding her hand and looking into her eyes, which were large and almost liquid. She seemed as fragile as a bubble and as strong as a monument that day, in a deep state of surrender to her current state of physical existence. Our interaction was a gift and a lesson in surrendering to the way things are. I visited Eileen only once more before she managed her peaceful transition. About a week later, I returned to the house and met her husband and her sister. They showed me pictures of Eileen taken before her illness. I gave them a copy of the words I had written about my relationship with her. We spoke about flowers and families. I knew it was highly unlikely I would ever see either of them again, yet they felt like friends. I wished them well, we hugged goodbye, and I marveled at how affected I'd been by the short amount of time I had spent with their loved one.

> Our acquaintance seemingly brief
> inside a timeless sacred space
> I will remember You.
> I will remember your hand
> resting gracefully on a pillow
> your beautiful long fingers
> with manicured nails
> peach colored just like your blanket.
> I will remember your eyes meeting mine
> as we sat together in hallowed silence.
> I will remember you allowing me to
> touch and warm the body
> you were soon to leave behind.
> I will remember you making
> the effort to speak to tell me
> the touch felt good and to
> thank me for coming.
> Yet it is I who must thank you
> for your gift of sharing
> with me, a fellow traveler,
> those simple truthful moments
> in the journey of your life.

The second individual who came into my life by virtue of being enrolled in a hospice care program was a gentleman in his mid 70s. He and his wife lived in a double wide trailer in an attractive, well established mobile home park.

Bob suffered from a rare neuromuscular disorder that causes constant and severe muscle contractions, most notably in the area of the neck and shoulders. Mary shared that her husband was nearly always in pain as she led me into his bedroom to introduce us. I noticed immediately that Bob's face was distorted from the continuous jerking of his neck to one side and that there was also a near constant twitching around his eyes. The rest of his body was close to immobile with his right arm, neck and shoulder frozen into a contorted position, which impeded his ability to speak clearly. His wife pragmatically pointed out the various tubes attached to her husband's body, explaining what each one was for. A portable aspiration machine sat on a bedside table. There was oxygen at the ready. My mind rebelled at the toll this unusual disease had exacted on this gentleman's physical body, as well as on his and his wife's lives. However, I understood that I was being given an opportunity to keep my attention on Bob as an individual rather than on his physical struggle.

I visited Bob weekly at first and then twice weekly for a period of seven months leading up to his death. He seemed to enjoy and appreciate the lotion and gentle massage on his feet and legs. I eventually found ways to access his upper back and shoulders and he was able to relax enough to ease a bit of the rigidity in his neck. It became easier to understand whatever Bob was expressing verbally by focusing on him rather than on the words he had such difficulty articulating.

I eventually learned that Bob's condition was exacerbated and accelerated a few years before we met by an error their pharmacy made in filling a prescription. The dosage turned out to be way stronger than was stated on the label. He and his wife chose not to sue the pharmacy, nor did they change their HMO. Clearly, they had not let this catastrophic incident turn them into angry or vindictive people or get in the way of their commitment to each other. Their ability to focus on the positive, no matter what each day or night might bring, was incredibly inspiring.

Over time, Bob was able to relax enough during our weekly sessions together so that he could breathe more easily. Eventually he was also able to fall asleep without any of his medications aimed at that result. His kind-hearted wife, who proclaimed this achievement miraculous, felt relaxed enough herself to run short errands while I was with Bob.

Not long after I began visiting Bob, the Director of the Hospice program I was volunteering for at that time received a letter from Mary, and he gave me a copy. In her letter, Mary outlined how much her husband was benefiting from my visits, practically insisting that I be paid and pleading for me to be allowed to come twice a week. Her suggestion in the last paragraph of her letter that she felt certain they could surely find some money in their donated funds to pay for the service, made me suspect she had enclosed a contribution for such a fund. I was then paid a small stipend which gradually increased over the years, for each person I visited from that time forward. As word spread that this amenity, along with music and other complimentary therapies was available, more and more requests were being made. Happily, I was eventually to be able to bring in a couple other people I had trained to help meet those wishes.

In the meantime, my daughter was carving out a career for herself working in residential care facilities. She mentioned one day that residents in the extended care center where she was then serving as Social Services Director could certainly benefit from the type of support that I was offering to hospice patients. She pointed out that some family members would likely be happy to pay for that kind of amenity, adding that residents on Medi-Cal, the California equivalent of Medicaid, received a small discretionary monthly stipend that often went unspent. Inspired by my daughter's idea, I created COMPASSIONATE TOUCH for Those in Later Life Stages™ in order to reach out to groups of people who are often marginalized in our society, especially and specifically, the frail elderly, the chronically ill, and those nearing death. I wanted to serve those who are less mobile, who might be confined to wheelchairs or beds, and those alienated from the outside world, whether in their own homes or in care communities. I hoped to offer gentle massage and intentional touch to individuals who might be physically touched as part of routine caregiving, or in the course of medical tests and procedures, yet who were seldom if ever receiving the kind of nurturing, unconditional contact that I knew could be enormously comforting, and healing in the deepest sense.

I quickly discovered that my visits were particularly needed and especially appreciated by those unable to clearly articulate their needs, whether that was due to a brain insult such as Alzheimer's Disease or other types of dementia, an inability to make themselves understood in English, or because the person had simply given up trying to talk when it became clear that nobody was really listening. Human hearts of all ages and in all situations yearn for acceptance, affection and authentic human connection. When words fail, touch continues the conversation. Intentional, yet non-invasive physical contact offers comfort, support and assurance that a person is not alone.

The significance of the attentive listening part of the dyad format on Enlightenment Intensives was just as obvious in relating to the elderly and ill individuals. In his book, *No More Secondhand Art*, Peter London writes about the attributes of a good listener and exhorts us to "hear every word, every inflection, every silence." He talks about hearing not only with our ears, "but with your skin, your fingers, your heart" and urges us to be present with no agenda "other than full, undivided, patient attention." I learned that the most productive and effective path to compassion is to open to and receive each individual's communications in exactly that way.

As I began visiting residents in nursing homes and in dementia care units, I was amazed at the number of positive indicators I received. I soon discovered that focused, conscious touch—along with open-hearted presence, and attentive listening—had enormous potential to ease discomfort, to calm the mind and to lift the spirits of these less mobile and confined individuals. I learned that those who don't answer questions quickly enough or who may not respond to what they hear as repetitive or perfunctory comments, without actual personal contact, from a busy caregiver such as "How are we feeling today?" or "Are you ready for your bath?" are often too quickly assumed to be nonverbal. Once that notation is in the resident's chart, other caregivers often stop making any effort to elicit a response.

Something completely unexpected came to light one morning while I was spending time with a rather regal looking lady in her mid-eighties who was living out her years in a long-term care facility. This tall, bone-thin, wheel-chair bound woman had not spoken a word during the several months I had been seeing her regularly, although after only a few bi-monthly visits, she had begun to make eye contact and return my smile as I was sitting beside her applying lotion to her hands and lower arms. Eventually, she began to visibly relax in responding to gentle massage on her shoulders and upper back. During my next visit, completely out of the blue, this formerly silent elder said quite clearly as if we were in the middle of a friendly conversation, "My husband and I used to go dancing." Startled, yet delighted to hear her speak, I immediately sat down beside her. As our eyes met, I asked where she and her husband went to dance. She then described the venue in detail, and went on to answer, with increasing enthusiasm, a few more of my queries. Grateful to know that she could still retrieve pleasant memories and share them, and that she trusted me with her words that morning, I was reluctant to leave her room. I never again let a designation of "nonverbal "in someone's medical chart speak for itself. It was not the last time I discovered the label to be an error.

My experience in spending time on a near daily basis for several years with my mother, Ruth Ann, and later, my mother-in-law, as each woman moved away from a home that she had lived in for decades to assisted living, to nursing care, to board and care, and eventually, to hospice care, afforded me a number of new insights. I also gained a much greater awareness of the vicissitudes of life for those who have little control over their environments—the sounds, the sights, the smells, the schedule—and who become powerless to change their situations. Being present with each of these women in the last stages of a long life, and as each drew her last breath, was an additional gift.

Mother Theresa once declared, "We shall never know all the good that a simple smile can do." It is not unusual to see residents in care facilities, lying in their beds, or sitting in their rooms or in hallways, virtually unnoticed and ignored by busy and often over-worked and underpaid caregivers. "Just waiting . . . waiting . . . waiting," a resident in her wheelchair opposite the nurse's station once uttered softly when I stopped to ask her how she was doing that day. I didn't ask her what she was waiting for. It might have been for the next meal, for a loved one to visit, or to be taken back to her room. I have come to realize, however, that quite often facility residents like her are often simply waiting—sometimes for what must seem like hours—for someone to smile at them, to say hello, to call them by name, or to simply acknowledge their existence in some small way. My gradual familiarity with a number of those residents provided me with indisputable evidence of the efficacy of mindful and unconditional contact, of stopping even briefly to say hello and shake a gentlemen's hand, to give someone a sincere compliment ("your blue shirt matches the color of your eyes" or "your hair looks nice today"). It is such an easy yet significant gesture to simply take even a few minutes to listen to what someone might want to communicate, without an agenda, without evaluating, without giving advice or administering medications. We really have no idea how much some small act of kindness may mean to another human being.

People of any age who are nearing the end of their lives can feel abandoned in a multitude of ways as they begin experiencing never-to-be reversed losses, sometimes in quick succession. Such individuals may unexpectedly find themselves in a care facility for any number of reasons. Some need rehabilitation after an injury; others need short-term care while recovering from surgery. Others have been relocated because family members believe their loved ones can no longer live alone safely, or because they have no family members who are both able and willing to provide the kind of support that a loved one has come to need.

Regardless of the reasons for such a move, leaving one's home and familiar surroundings represents a major lifestyle change. That aging or ill individual is suddenly bereft of familiar surroundings, relegated to rules and timetables for everything from food service to entertainment and group activities, all of which are based on management efficiency and the convenience of administrators and staff members rather than on individual preferences, habits, rhythms, and tastes. Stress, anxiety, and depression are common reactions in such communities. Residents are more often than not treated with prescription drugs which, in turn, have their own side effects.

I remember fondly a cheerful, wheelchair-bound elderly woman I spent a bit of time with once a week at a respite care center, one of the more alert and talkative of the participants in the program. She particularly liked the little finger puppets I brought to share with a few people from time to time, and she usually greeted me with a big smile. One day, even before sitting down beside her, I noticed that she seemed to be upset about something. When I touched her arm and asked her what was wrong, she whispered tearfully, "I don't live in my house anymore." I kept my attention on her, holding her hand until she continued. She then told me that, without giving her any warning, her daughters were moving her into "one of those facilities." According to her, they had told her she would be there for just a few days, and then she discovered the move was to be permanent.

When I was able to get permission to visit this woman in the nursing home she'd been moved to, I found her struggling to adjust to a completely new, unfamiliar environment among strangers. She was, understandably, feeling confined, with only a few of her personal belongings in a much smaller space than she was used to, and which she was sharing with a woman she'd never met before. She mentioned that her roommate kept her awake at night with her loud snoring. From her point of view, she'd had no say in the decision that was made on her behalf. I validated what she was feeling and told her I was sorry. Realizing that I was privy to a very small part of what was likely a much larger story, I tried not to judge her daughters. The next time I stopped by to say hello, I found her bed empty and when I inquired as to her whereabouts, the nurse pointed toward the ceiling. My first thought was to wonder why had she had been moved to another floor?" Was it because of her roommate's snoring? Had her daughters been able to get her a private room? When I asked what her new room number was, I was told she had died. As startled and saddened as I was to have missed seeing her again, I had to smile, remembering that there was no second floor in that nursing home.

From my present perspective, I can see that my childhood experience of being placed in an institutional care setting, with little understanding or power over the situation, instantly relegated to life among strangers in an unfamiliar environment, provided a context for empathy and compassion to germinate and grow in me. I realized much later that the fulfillment I receive from relating to those in the later stages of life comes from my ability to offer the support I did not have during that confusing, lonely and vulnerable time in my early childhood. I don't have the ability to change a person's circumstances or condition. I cannot be a "savior." I am unable to reverse an aging or a disease process, nor can I change a medical system or a family dynamic. What I can do is be in contact with and acknowledge the individual and be present with them. I can remain conscious, open and kind during whatever time we spend together.

In my years of working regularly with those nearing death, I was often particularly moved by my encounters with those who were suffering from AIDS. Not all were male nor were they all gay yet, invariably, they were much younger than other people I visited more frequently. Often in their twenties or thirties, some were angry, some were afraid, some were bitter. Many were isolated and lonely.

One young man I spent time with had been abandoned by both parents and his two brothers, due to his "lifestyle choices." When I met him, he was withdrawn and dispirited. Beneath his depression, I could see a scared young boy missing his mother, longing for acceptance from his father, and mourning the loss of companionship he might have had with his brothers. After only a few visits, he told me he was ready to die, and that he wished he could speed up the process. I knew from the 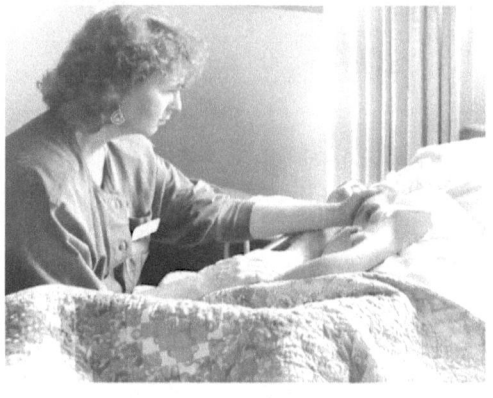 one sibling who had remained in his life, the sister who was caring for him, that their mother—in defiance of her husband—was planning on coming to visit him. I gently suggested maybe he could give his mom a chance. I happened to be the only other person in the home the day his mother arrived at the front door, suitcase in hand. She was so clearly distressed and anxious as she stepped into the house that I spontaneously hugged her. As she held me tightly for a long minute, I felt her enormous sorrow as well as the courage it took for her to be there. We shared a few words, one mother to another, before I ushered her into the room where her son lay in his bed, emaciated and distant. I always hoped that they were able to achieve some form of reconciliation in the three days they had together before that particular mother's life-weary child let go of his body.

Logan/David

They said you might be difficult,
might not accept massage if offered ...
yet it seemed you couldn't get enough
of touching, or of talking
each time I came to see you.
They said that you were angry.
They were right, of course
yet underneath your anger
was a scared little boy
crying for his mother
to make this bad thing go away
yearning for a father
who could somehow accept him
lonely for the brothers
he felt had betrayed him,
grieving for the friends
who had already died.
I learned that you had changed your name
"to protect the innocent " you said
grasping at the edge of bitterness
for a piece of understanding
while longing for respect.
The mental monsters were turning
your dreams to nightmares that
raged and ravaged, battling on
until your body slowly weakened
and in the end, exhausted,
you gave up the fight.
You were ready to die you said,
the day your mother finally came,
love swallowing her terror,
to spend two weeks with you.
You gave her three days only for
the seven years she'd missed,
finding, at last, a way to forgive her
and—just maybe—all the others too?

As the well-known author and physician Rachel Naomi Remen has written, "It is our wounds that enable us to be compassionate with the wounds of others." I know now that choosing to interact with men and women who are often secluded, feeling alone and lonely, has been a significant influence in helping me heal from those early periods of my life when I experienced a number of the same feelings—when I was vulnerable, uneasy and anxious, when I longed to be noticed and heard, when I was in need of acknowledgement, nourishing touch, and caring attention. The simplest, yet all too often ignored acts of kindness, compassion, and authentic contact can deeply affect both the giver and the receiver. Even a few moments of deep listening, combined with nonintrusive, gentle touch, can truly make a difference. I have witnessed this countless times over the years. Every individual I have been privileged to meet during this unique period in their lives has taught me something new about myself, about life, about aging, about death, about love, about surrender. The emotional effects and notable lessons from many of those interactions are detailed in my book, *From the Heart Through the Hands: The Power of Touch in Caregiving*. Suffice it to say that a few situations have been mentally and emotionally draining. Some have been intense, initially awkward or uncomfortable, while others were relaxing, tranquil, inspiring. Some of the environments I've encountered have been cluttered and chaotic while others were calm, peaceful spaces. I visited a few individuals only once or twice. Others I spent time with regularly for weeks or months or, in a few instances, over a year or longer. Sometimes other family members were present and were included in my sessions; other times the person I was sent to see was alone.

Interacting with those who are nearing the transition we refer to as death has been a profound growth experience that has challenged me, changed me, and brought me into deeper contact with my true

Self. It has given me the chance to spend time with individuals ranging in age from five years to 101 whom I would otherwise never have met. It has given me the opportunity to surrender my ego, to trust my instincts and to rise above fatigue or fear in order to be present with and for another human being during a fragile and vulnerable time in that person's life. It has allowed me to experience both the strength and the fragility of life, to look more deeply into my own fears about death and dying, and to notice my resistances to meeting life as it is. The scores of individuals approaching death who have invited me to touch their bodies, to listen to their stories or to sit awhile with them and share their precious time have enriched my life, expanded my awareness of impermanence, and deepened my capacity for compassion. It has reminded me that we can find indescribable sweetness in unexpected people and places to the extent that we are open to the way things are, and that every moment of life and death is holy.

My stepmother, Ruth Ann, also known as Ruth, Ruthie, or occasionally R.A., once told me that her parents had almost named her Esther.

Eleven

Forgiving Esther

The way we talk to our children becomes their inner voice.
~ Peggy O'Mara

Forgiveness is the necessary ground for any healing. Sometimes it's quick and sometimes it takes a lifetime.
~ Jack Kornfield

Forgive Esther for what exactly? one might ask. For starters, for the humiliation, the emotional blackmail, for harassing, haranguing, criticizing and "opinionating" me to death; for forever trying to make me be something better, something else, something more, or something different from what I was; for the incessant—and I do mean incessant, as in constant, continuous, unending, ceaseless, interminable, perpetual and everlasting—preachy harping; for the seemingly endless stream of words that poured out of her mouth, infiltrating my being, clogging every pore in my body until I could hardly breathe, filling every mental air pocket in my brain until my own embryonic thoughts were suffocated mid-birth.

Nearly every day that Esther and I spent together in the same house, I went to sleep to the sound of her voice and awoke to the same sound whether she was talking to me, to someone else, or to herself. It didn't seem to matter to her if people were listening to what she was saying or if they talked back. When she asked a question, she seemed unable to keep her mouth from moving long enough to listen to the answer.

During my youth, one of the few times Esther stopped talking was when she was sunbathing. It was as if the heat incinerated her words before they could escape from her mouth. On sunny days she would rush home from her secretarial job, set up the folding aluminum and vinyl chaise lounge in our small backyard, take off her blouse, pull up her skirt, and stretch out to catch whatever rays she could. After a friend told her that putting a drop or two of iodine in Johnson's Baby Oil was the best way to get a fast tan, she religiously applied this potion to her exposed skin. In lieu of sunglasses, Esther placed wet, flattened cotton balls over her eyelids. I never knew if she was asleep under those white pallets, mulling over plans for the future, or simply day dreaming. As the days shortened in the fall, Esther had less and less time in the sun, but when spring moved towards summer, my respite from her words might lengthen to an hour or more.

Apart from talking, Esther's favorite pastime seemed to be clothes shopping. As a child, I was often forced to accompany Esther on long and tedious excursions in which I became her "runner," making endless trips between the dressing room and the racks to exchange one piece of clothing for another in a different size or color. Like most decisions Esther made, choosing which items to purchase was never quick or simple. Her choices came only after a long, meandering, incomprehensible-to-anyone-but-her dialogue that Esther's mind carried on, sometimes out loud, with itself.

Esther's presence in any department store inevitably meant there was a sale in progress. Picture gaggles of women of all ages, shapes and sizes hell-bent on snatching the best possible deal before anyone else could grab it, descending like birds of prey on the pocketed wooden tables filled with seasonal attire, pecking at whatever bits of color or fabric caught their fancy until the neatly ordered piles turned into one big blur of tossed and tousled material. Clutching their prizes in brightly polished talons as if their lives depended on it, the crazed creatures then moved quickly to the racks of dresses, slacks, or skirts, their minds and eyes intently focused on the hunt, their squawks turning shrill as they competed with each other for the attention of the sales girls or argued with shopping partners about the merits of one color or style over another. This escalating vocal cacophony, combined with the distinctive whoosh of the cash stuffed tubes moving through the pneumatic tube system on their way to the cashiers, created a din that assailed the senses of anyone not involved in the frenzy.

I once sought refuge in the center of a large circular rack only to discover a like-minded young person. The pig-tailed, freckle-faced girl forgave me for invading her secret cave, grinning conspiratorially as we both hid from the madding crowd. We sat smugly and silently, like two escapees from Leavenworth as the garments swished and whirled around us until we were discovered, duly chastised, and dragged off by our forearms, in opposite directions.

Occasionally, two women—one of them being Esther—would reach for the same item at the exact same time. When this occurred, Esther would resort to one of two tactics. The first was to declare, in a cloyingly sweet yet raised voice, "Oh, I'm so sorry dear, but I had this first," while smiling meaningfully and keeping a firm grip on the item until the other woman dropped her end. Her alternate strategy was to accost the offending shopper in a loud, accusing tone: "Hey, what are you trying to pull? You saw me reaching for this one!" or "You know I had this first!" The accompanying facial expression was a piercing, beady-eyed look under furrowed brows. If all else failed, Esther would just give an unexpected yank and end the contest.

Once Esther managed to make up her mind regarding which items of clothing she wanted, there was still the line to wait through before her selections could be purchased or put on layaway. As I stood beside Esther in the row of chattering women, she would invariably spot some garment she hadn't noticed before in her mad dash through the racks, or become plagued with doubt about a choice she'd made, and I was left to hold her place in line while she rushed back into the fray. Whether due to my height, my age or my silence, the buyers behind me in the ever- lengthening queue usually ignored me as if I was wearing an invisibility cloak as they continued their forward movement. More often than not, Esther was so preoccupied with her own thoughts that she failed to notice I had gained little if any ground by the time she returned.

The annual Henry's Clothing and Shoe Store event held every December seemed to excite Esther at least as much as Christmas. Esther never missed this chance to save money and stock up on shoes, most of which she would never wear. At that point in her life, Esther could dazzle, bewitch, or seduce nearly any man into giving her whatever she wanted with a simple turn of her head and an enigmatic smile. I watched, with a mixture of fascination and embarrassment, as she flirted with the young salesmen sitting on their wooden shoe-fitting stools in front of her, easing her silk stockinged feet into shoe after shoe. With each new offering, Esther would parade before them, inviting their thoughts as to which pair of shoes looked better. The quick-witted salesmen would say that every shoe looked so good on her, they just couldn't decide, at which point Esther would laugh playfully and say if that were the case, she supposed she'd just have to take both pairs, and two more boxes would be added to the growing stack.

Racing towards thirteen, I was wearing my recently acquired real bra, desperately wishing I was older and sitting anywhere other than the passenger side of Esther's old black Plymouth sedan, when she abruptly made one of her impulsive stops "even though there is no sale going on" at a local department store. Once inside, Esther waved me over to the section displaying clothing that might soon fit my quickly changing body, telling me I could "browse" for a few minutes. The navy-blue skirt stood out like a jewel in gravel. There were few people in that area of the store that weeknight, and no sales girl in sight as I lifted the hanger from its rack and boldly headed for a dressing- room. This remarkable piece of clothing, a fitted skirt made of some sort of seductively soft yet durable material, fit perfectly around my newly forming hips. The smooth, silk-like lining caressed my legs when I moved. Words cannot describe the sensations I experienced gazing at my image in the full-length mirror. It was as if the skirt possessed some supernatural power that made me appear not only older but prettier, smarter, happier. I begged Esther to buy it for me and in the end, most likely distracted by her own decision-making process, she consented.

I wore the magical garment to the next Wednesday night prayer meeting at our church. Esther sat down near the back and, without waiting for permission, I walked all the way up to the front pews where the pre-teen children were encouraged to sit. I could literally feel both the song leader and the preacher looking at me differently. The boy who would become my "first kiss" a few months later came right up to me at the end of the service and mumbled something I chose to hear as a prelude to romance.

The next day, without warning or discussion, Esther removed the skirt from my closet and returned it to the store. I never knew the exact reason she changed her mind, but I hated her for the betrayal, and I vowed I would never forgive her. Perhaps she felt somehow threatened by my emerging sexuality. Maybe noticing how people had glanced at me made her feel she'd be judged in some way. Or, just possibly, it nudged Esther into the realization that I was growing up and would one day move beyond her control. She needn't have worried. Her invasion of my psyche was so complete that it took me decades to begin actually thinking for myself.

As I neared my mid-teens, Esther seemed to be becoming more and more religious, my father was spending more and more time out of town, and I was on the receiving of Esther's frustration and resentment. Thankfully, I was allowed to attend a boarding school in another state to escape the fallout when my father took his leave of Esther and began spending more time with the woman who would become his fourth and final wife.

With my father and me both gone, Esther sought prayers and counseling. Many years later she told me that the therapist she had a few sessions with kept telling her, "You don't want to be with a man who doesn't love you!" and that she kept saying, "Yes, I do want to be with him. I love him. I only want to be with him!" Eventually rallying after what was referred to as her nervous breakdown, she flew to Paris to visit a friend, and procured a Civil Service job that kept her living abroad for two decades. Far away from her former life, Esther fell off the church pew and reinvented herself. By changing her hair color, the way she dressed, and the birthdate on her passport, she was able to successfully present herself as ten years younger than she actually was. Esther learned to ski, traveled to other countries every chance she got, and dated a steady stream of men of varying ages.

∞

When Esther retired from her overseas job, over twenty years later, and moved back to the town where we had once lived together, she sent me a plane ticket to come visit her. She insisted on spending the first day of my three-day visit going to the end-of-summer department store sales. Her habits little changed, she draped my arms with "outfits" for one of us to try on, chirping on in a mostly one-way conversation about what tops went best with which bottoms. Digging through the sales bins at a frenzied pace, something that had surely always been inevitable occurred. Esther and another sales addicted woman grabbed a gauzy, white blouse at the same moment. Like two birds with one worm, they each yanked and the material ripped. There was a brief hush, in a stop-motion millisecond, before the other shoppers quickly dispersed. Apparently at a loss for words—for possibly the second time in her life—Esther quickly released her grip on the material and strode silently toward the nearest store exit, with me at her heels.

Esther's conversion to a radically different way of shopping was swift. Secondhand stores offered the ultimate, never-ending sale, and they were seldom overcrowded. In the years to come, Esther's Christmas boxes arrived filled with carefully wrapped and ribboned gifts of pre-owned clothing that might or might not fit anyone in our family, children's books with a torn or missing page, jigsaw puzzles absent the final piece, or toys lacking some crucial part. During Esther's visits "out west," perusing our local thrift shops was high on her agenda. It mattered little to Esther if the clothes she bought were her size. If something caught her eye or appealed to her in any way, she'd snatch it, deciding later what to keep for herself and what to give to someone else. I learned to simply thank Esther for any purchases passed on to me or my family, taught my children to do the same, and donated most of the items back to the same thrift store later.

Esther's long distance telephone conversations were no different from those she carried on in person. I once prepared an entire meal during one of her seemingly unlimited calls. When I needed both hands, I set the telephone receiver down on the kitchen counter, leaning over every so often to murmur, "Hmm," "Oh?" or "Really!" This was about all that was required from my end for nearly an hour.

As destiny or fate would have it, I chose to take responsibility for Esther's care and well-being during what turned out to be the last two years of her life. When I suggested a move to California, and to an assisted living community near our house, she told everyone in the midwestern nursing home—where she had been living an underactive and overmedicated life—that she was going to "the land of sunshine," where fresh fruit and vegetables were plentiful year-round, to be nearer to her grandchildren and to meet "my grand dogs and grand cats!"

Age had begun taking its toll on Esther, although she could still talk a blue streak on a good day once she got started. She became stooped and her gait was unsteady until she finally accepted the 4-wheeled walker the physical therapist I'd engaged to see her prescribed, something she had sworn she would never use. Esther loved visiting the dog and cats in our home on weekends. She thrived on the attention bestowed upon her in the Assisted Living spaces, making no distinction between her fellow residents in the building—including a large, docile cat—and the caregivers, befriending them all. She was thrilled with the variety of food served in the well-appointed dining room, especially the desserts. Ignoring her infirmities, Esther flirted up a storm, sweet-talking the male servers assigned to her table just as she had the young men in Henry's shoe department decades before. Although her early charm and charisma had diminished some as she grew older, she had no trouble cajoling an eager-to-please young man into bringing her extra ice-cream or second servings of her favorite pies. She once advised the head chef, who strolled through the dining room every so often exuding a certain glib charm, that a bit of lemon juice on the steamed spinach would improve the taste, adding with a coquettish laugh, that serving it with fried potatoes and onions would make it perfect.

A couple of times, I attended a particularly interesting group activity with Esther, along with a half dozen other elderly women seated in a circle on straight-backed chairs. The young woman in charge would begin singing a familiar hymn and most of the people in the circle would immediately join in. Esther always sat up straight and brightened immediately, singing every hymn in a confident, strong voice. As I sang along with her, it was as if the years had disappeared and we were transported back in time. I often wished there could have been such an activity every day. Studies on this subject have revealed that choral singing can enhance overall psychological well-being. Singing along with others causes the brain to secrete oxytocin, a naturally occurring hormone that can alleviate chronic pain or sensations of anxiety. I've read articles attesting to the fact that endorphins and dopamine released during group singing help strengthen neural pathways and increase neuroplasticity—the brain's ability to change and adapt. The power of music has been shown to have particularly remarkable effects in the treatment of dementia as well as trauma.

After a middle of the night fall when she tried to get out of bed without help and wasn't discovered by anyone for several hours, Esther underwent surgery for a broken hip. She then had to be moved to a nearby nursing home that included an active rehabilitation component. I came most days during the lunch hour, often bringing foods I knew Esther liked, to coax her into eating more. No longer able to speak and consume food at the same time, Esther predictably chose talking over eating.

On warm days, I'd push her in her wheelchair outside after lunch so she could sit in the sunshine she loved. She often pointed out things I hadn't noticed—birds frolicking in the courtyard fountain or gathered to gossip on a rooftop, unusual cloud shapes, a butterfly dining on salvia, or an iris about to unfurl. When she tired, Esther would simply close her eyes and turn her face toward the sun.

Esther spoke less and less as the months passed, sometimes going silent for long periods. Incredibly, I found myself missing the sound of her voice. Asking her questions brought limited responses, although bringing in pictures of her ancestors prompted stories I'd never heard before. Peering at those age-old black and white photographs seemed to jump-start her mind. She would immediately begin describing the colors of the flowers in the background or details about the materials in the dress her "Mama stayed up nearly all-night sewing" for her. Pausing one day, mid-sentence, a puzzled look crossed Esther's face. "Where are my sisters now?" she asked, as if she just realized she had misplaced something precious. I searched my mind for an answer that would reassure rather than upset her.

"Why, they're in heaven, waiting for you, I expect."

"Oh, yes," Esther replied, smiling at me with such childlike innocence that I couldn't look away.

"I love you, Mother." I heard myself say earnestly. Esther responded as if she might have been asking what day it was.

"Am I your mother?"

"Yes," I replied, with long-delayed certainty, and unexpected emotion, you are my mother." The smile that appeared on Esther's face, the look in her eyes at that moment, was sweetness itself. I let my tears fall. I experienced a rush of heat over my entire body. And then, something extraordinary occurred. It was as if Esther and I were suddenly in that field that mystics talk about, out beyond wrong doing and right doing. There was nothing to forgive. There was nothing but love in my heart. There was nothing but Love, period. About a month later, my mother died in my arms as I sang one of her favorite hymns about Jesus calling her home. I substituted the word *loved one* for *sinner* in the chorus: "Softly and tenderly, Jesus is calling, calling, oh loved one, come home."

Twelve

Goddess Descending: The Larger Story.

We are healed when we can grow from our suffering, when we can reframe it as an act of grace that leads us back to who we truly are.

~ Joan Borysenko

Soul making requires that you die to one story to be reborn to a larger one.

~ Jean Houston

In an exercise entitled "Healing the Sacred Wound" in Jean Houston's groundbreaking work, *The Search for the Beloved,* one is asked to focus on a significant upheaval or distress in her life, to answer certain questions about the event, and then to reimagine and rewrite the story by assuming the role of mythmaker, using archetypal images. Completing this assignment for a graduate class I was taking was the beginning of a shift in my perspective regarding my preverbal and developmental childhood trauma.

I

In the realm of Eternal Light, there lived a Goddess known as Eos, the Goddess of the Rising Sun. After giving the matter a great deal of thought, Eos approached Hera, Queen of the Heavenly Realms with a request that she be sent to a planet called Earth in the form of a human being.

"For what purpose?" she was asked.

"I want to understand Sorrow and Joy. I want to learn about Suffering, Eos explained, "and I have heard that human beings suffer most of all."

"Are you willing to stay on the Planet of Sorrows, in a human body, and experience whatever is necessary to learn what you wish to?" asked the Queen of Heavenly Realms.

"I am," replied Eos.

"Then I will grant your wish, but I will need to find one willing to make the sacrifice to assist in this most difficult task."

The Goddess of the Rising Sun, who was not known for her patience, said resolutely, "I will wait."

It came to pass that Leto, the Goddess of Motherhood, volunteered to fulfill the request of Hera to help teach the Goddess of the Rising Sun about Suffering, Sorrow, and Joy. Hera admonished Eos, who was often found floating dreamily in the heavenly realms while creating new light, to *Stay Awake and Pay Attention!* "Although your father on Earth will become very important to you later in your life, it is the one who has consented to give birth to you in human form who will be the first to help teach you that which you seek to learn.

II

And so it was that the Goddess of the Rising Sun arrived on the planet called Earth, born through the body of a young female Earthling whose name was Grace. Becoming human was not easy. It required a long, uncomfortable struggle through a dark and narrow tunnel which seemed to cause the Earth woman great pain. As the Goddess of the Rising Sun tried to push her way out of the tunnel, she could feel resistance and fear surrounding the tunnel.

The human giving birth was put into a deep sleep so that she missed her baby's entrance onto the planet called Earth. She did not recognize the infant who emerged from her body as who she actually was. The new Mother felt only disappointment when she realized what she had given birth to was a girl instead of the male child she thought she wanted. She resented the pain that she had endured, and she was angry that the father of her child was far away in *The War* instead of being there with her. She wasn't even sure why she decided to call the infant Dawn, though something deep inside her seemed to reminded her of a task she had been given to carry out.

III

The Goddess of the Rising Sun become human was dependent on the Earth woman whose body she had emerged from to love and protect her, feed her, and keep her clean and warm, yet the human woman left her all alone much of the time. The baby called Dawn cried out when she was wet or cold or hungry for that is all her small body could do. Maybe the Earth woman couldn't hear her. When she cried louder, sometimes the woman came to the platform girded on all sides that humans called a crib, and lifted her out, yet many times no one came.

In due time, she was able to turn her small body over, and to move a little on her hands and knees. After a few more months of human time, she began trying to imitate some of the words human beings use to communicate with one another, which seemed to please her human Mother.

It came to pass during the time Earth beings call Autumn, that the human mother left her baby alone once again after darkness fell. This time, she was not there when the dark faded into light and then back to dark again. The human baby called Dawn was trapped and could do nothing to help herself. She cried as long and as loud as she could, yet nobody came. There was only darkness and light and then darkness once again. Each time she awoke she was hungrier and colder. As light turned to darkness once again, she grew weaker, and somewhere inside her, a feeling began to form that she had done something wrong. She began to lose touch with her small human body. Her energy waned and she could make no sound when the strangers came and found her. A kind woman quickly put clean clothing on her and wrapped her in a blanket before rushing her to a large space with bright lights and strange noises. After several days in this unfamiliar place, she was taken to the home of her Earth Father's parents, where she was loved and nurtured and eventually began to thrive under her grand-parents' devoted, tender care. As she learned to walk and talk a little, she seemed to forget the dark wound in her soul and being forsaken by the woman who was her mother; yet the Goddess become mortal had a long journey ahead of her.

IV

In the course of Earth time, the human named Dawn grew into a woman. She came together with a human male who was good and kind and whom she promised to love and honor. She trusted that she was fulfilling her destiny on Earth. When she became a mother herself, the love she felt for the two beings who came through her body was greater than any she had ever known. If one of them suffered, she experienced the pain as her own and she also suffered.

Even though she made mistakes, the human on Earth called Dawn tried as hard as she could to be a good wife and a good mother. When the life she was certain she was destined to live changed course, she believed she had failed and that she alone was to blame. She even thought that she did not deserve to be alive, yet her life on Earth continued. When she remembered the story about her first year of life and thought about the woman who had abandoned her, there was a deep sorrow inside her that never truly went away. She was convinced that she was not worthy of True Love.

Leto, the Goddess of Motherhood, who had left the Heavenly Realms to help fulfill the request of the Goddess of the Rising Sun, lived a difficult life struggling with remorse, guilt, and the demons of addiction. Her heart was often heavy. After leaving her human body and returning to the Heavenly Realms, Leto was congratulated by Hera for the great skill she had displayed in carrying out her difficult assignment on the Planet of Sorrows known as Earth.

V

On the planet called Earth, it came to pass that the Goddess of the Rising Sun become human was united with another male Earthling who was persistent and determined in his quest to prove his unwavering love and support. In the fullness of time, they came together as life partners. When the human called Dawn felt a deep yearning to give birth to one more child in her lifetime and her aging body rejected two beings sent into her womb, her Sorrow was great. The earnest supplications of Eos in her human form and her promise to pay close attention and to learn all that she could if she was allowed to give birth to one more child moved Hera, Queen of the Heavenly Realms.

When Leto, the Goddess of Motherhood approached Hera and asked to return to Earth one more time, both wishes were granted. The Queen of the Heavenly Realm even sent her daughter, the Goddess of Pregnancy and Birth, to watch over and protect the human named Dawn until her child arrived safely on the planet called Earth.

And so, a new human life emerged, a radiant, pure and beautiful baby girl whose sweetness filled the room. The hearts of the human mother and father were opened and they were allowed to know that the child was a Divine being come to Earth to teach them something important. They honored her by remaining conscious of who she actually was, and by striving to be the best caretakers they possibly could, even when it was utterly fatiguing and their energy wavered.

As she grew, the child brought light and joy to the hearts of all who knew her. Her Mother thought that perhaps she was only able to appreciate the Joy she now felt because of the deep Sorrow carved into her being. She began to understand that she did deserve True Love and that it was actually something she had never been without.

The great wound began to heal. The Goddess of the Rising Sun become human on earth opened her heart more and more to her True Self, to the Eternal Goodness and Love that is. Leto, the Goddess of Motherhood who had asked to be re-born on Earth, was now released from her previous agreement to teach the Goddess of the Rising Sun about Suffering. She was now free to express fully and completely the great love she had always felt for the human on Earth she had once named Dawn.

Thirteen

Gratitude

If you concentrate on finding whatever is good, in every situation, you will discover that your life will suddenly be filled with gratitude . . .
~ Harold Kushner

Gratitude can transform any situation, moving you from negative energy to positive.
~ Oprah Winfrey

American psychologist, professor and author, Dr. Robert A. Emmons, a leading expert on the subject of gratitude, mentions in his introduction to The Little Book of Gratitude an article from Scientific American in 2015 reporting that out of twenty-four strengths, including love, hope, kindness and creativity, the single best predictor of good relationships and emotional well-being was gratitude. The myriad merits of practicing gratitude have been the subject of countless articles, books, workbooks, blogs and podcasts during the past decade. Ongoing research continues to uncover ways in which the intentional act of thanks giving, even when practiced as little as five minutes a day, can change both our brains and our lives.

An article appearing in 2023 on the website uclahealth.org mentions a review of seventy studies, including responses from more than 26,000 people, that found an association between higher levels of gratitude and lower levels of depression. Additional positive effects mentioned included helping lower blood pressure, boosting the immune system, improving self-esteem, enhancing empathy, strengthening relationships, reducing anxiety, helping people sleep better and lengthening life span. Gratitude may also play a major role in healing from trauma. The time taken to reflect on what we can be grateful for, whether it's an umbrella in a rainstorm, or the luxury of running water and a flushing toilet, contributes to a positive frame of mind as we go about the tasks of daily living. Giving thanks on a regular basis is a persuasive prescription for improving physical, mental, emotional, and spiritual health, while nurturing wholeness. In my experience, it has substantial and lasting effects.

My personal adult gratitude practice began when I spontaneously turned to that activity as a support during my first four-hour chemotherapy treatment after undergoing surgery for ovarian cancer in1998. Focusing on what I had to be grateful for was a godsend in the infusion room, when lying still for MRI or CT scans, or when I was trying to sleep in the middle of the night with peripheral neuropathy running rampant in my legs. That choice reinforced the lesson that the simple act of shifting our attention to something that is available to us, instead of thinking about what we don't have or cannot do, has tremendous power over the mind. When I was too weak to walk around the block, I could be grateful to make it down our long driveway to the mailbox; when I didn't have the energy to prepare a meal for my family, I was grateful I could fix myself a cup of hot tea or prepare a bowl of oatmeal for my breakfast.

During my illness, I became newly conscious of the long chain of hands and hearts that were contributing to my daily life and to my recovery, beginning with my medical team, my family, and the student turned friend who voluntarily drove down from Oregon to stay with us during my first week home from the hospital, seeing to our every need with singular generosity and compassion. My gratitude for the food cooked for us and delivered by different families every few days in the following weeks extended beyond being thankful for the time those friends took to prepare and bring the meals. I was thankful I was able to sit up in a chair at the table and that I could see, smell, chew, swallow and digest the food. I became aware of how many people—from the farm hands to the harvesters to the packers to the truck drivers to the store owners to the grocery clerks to those who purchased and prepared the food—were collectively responsible for those meals reaching my mouth, giving me nourishment helpful to my healing.

While I was slowly recovering my energy and brain power after my medical treatments ended, gratitude remained essential. Expressing gratitude for auxiliary therapies, for gifts of all kinds offered by family and friends in such loving and creative ways, as well as gifts from nature, from the universe and so on. Gratitude became a daily habit and an anchor for me. From that time forward, I began a mental list of things to be grateful for each morning, while still in bed. It took less than ten minutes to think of one hundred things to be grateful for though I soon quit keeping count of the number or the time. Gratitude helped calm my nerves on the way to the medical center for visits to my oncologist, during blood draws (especially when the needle didn't make its way into a vein on a first or second try) and for follow-up tests during that year.

Listing things I had to be grateful for during necessary dental procedures supported me in gradually releasing the stress and anxiety I had carried most of my life associated with going to the dentist. I often sang out my gratitude list on the drive to the dentist's office, and silently continued the list while in the chair, until the end of the procedure. Being able to listen to music or to an interview or speech on a headset had helped some. Eventually, however, it was the opportunity to engage in a prolonged gratitude practice that almost made me look forward to those dental appointments.

I have long remembered a lesson in gratitude I learned from a woman in her early thirties. As a result of a horseback riding accident a few years before we met, she was living out her life as a quadriplegic in a long-term care home. Her mobility was severely limited yet her spirit seemed as vast as the sky. The day I encountered her in the facility where I was giving a training workshop, she was reading a book, positioned on a special tray affixed to her chair. She was able, with concentrated effort, to turn the pages by using a device attached to her forehead. Her beautiful brown eyes smiled at me, even though her mouth could not. When I asked her if she had enjoyed the compassionate touch session from one of my students that day, she gave an enthusiastic, affirmative nod. Then, formulating the words slowly and with some difficulty, she said proudly, "Guess what? I can feel my legs!" The teaching she gave me in that moment in regard to focusing on what one has to be grateful for instead of on what has been irretrievably lost was priceless.

As my practice continued to deepen and expand, memories from my youth began surfacing, along with people whose names I'd long forgotten or situations I hadn't thought of in years. Names and images from my past began to appear in my consciousness like little lights twinkling in the darkness. I recognized that these were men and women who, in the trajectory of my life, had perceived something in me behind my usual façade. They were people who actually saw me: my fourth-grade classroom teacher; my Junior High homeroom teacher, my high school drama teacher; my college music teacher and his wife, a skillful and intuitive young therapist I'd had only a few sessions with years before. Though I wasn't aware of it at the time, their genuine contact and recognition made a difference. Each one of these individuals, in her or his own way, provided me with a stepping stone on a long path towards recovering my Self.

This daily exercise began taking me further and further back through the decades of my life, when suddenly an unexpected thought arose: "I am grateful to Penny, for carrying me inside her physical body for nine months and for going through the painful process of pushing me out through that body into this world." This recognition engendered an acute awareness of the fact that regardless of what happened after I was born, I would not be here today had she not given birth to me; and regardless of her persistent neglect during my first thirteen months of life, she did enough to keep me alive. I am grateful for that. I am grateful I didn't die. I am grateful to be alive. Soon after that I was able to experience and express gratitude for the fact that my birth mother drove from Florida to Kansas to meet me when I was seventeen. I am thankful to have met her when she was sober, grateful for my interactions with her a few more times across the years, particularly thankful to have survived our visit when her sobriety had lapsed without anything disastrous occurring. I am grateful she was able to "visit" me the night she left her body.

When I learned the name of the woman responsible for obtaining the search warrant that led to my discovery and rescue from my crib as an infant, Laurel Lyons was added to my gratitude list. Though

I'll never know their names, the neighbors who called social services to report a crying baby unattended in a darkened apartment—once again, perhaps—that particular night have also been added to my gratitude list. Gratitude isn't limited to a particular time or place. It can be practiced in nearly any setting: during dental procedures, sitting in a waiting room before a medical appointment, lying in a hospital bed waiting to be taken into the operating room, waiting for a stoplight to change from red to green, gazing through a window at a rose garden, or when having trouble falling asleep. Our gratitude lists can be generated silently in the mind or be voiced out loud, handwritten, typed and so on. The possibilities are unlimited.

My personal experience in this realm continued to deepen and expand as I shared it with loved ones, in group meetings, in friendship circles, and in training workshops. Now, when I begin to feel tense, overwhelmed, distracted, annoyed or irritable, if I simply inhale and exhale deeply once or twice, and sit quietly for a moment, and this soothing activity begins without effort. Gratitude has become a constant companion in the adventure we call aging as my physical and mental capacities are slowly declining and I can no longer accomplish all the things I could easily achieve or complete when I was younger. I wake up each morning grateful to be alive and mobile and my gratitude expands from there.

The act of expressing thanks helps support us as we navigate the multitude of unexpected challenges and changes in our lives, whether they are physical, medical, mental, emotional, or spiritual, whether it is a climate-related catastrophe, a worldwide pandemic blanketing our world, political chaos and uncertainty, or the sudden loss of a loved one altering our day-to-day reality. Gratitude can help us refocus when we become distracted and get lost inside thoughts about the past or the future. It can bring us back to the present moment, which is all we ever truly have. A consistent and purposeful acknowledgement of the gifts we so frequently take for granted, including the very fact of our embodied existence on this earth, enlarges our perspective and adds grace to our days. A long-time friend of mine recently said that by "cultivating gratitude, we develop our capacity to savor the immense richness, abundance, and potential of our brief and precious human life." For me personally, gratitude has become a habit of the heart and a primary spiritual practice.*

Breathing in I am alive. Breathing out I am grateful.

*See Appendix II for further suggestions on practicing gratitude.

Fourteen

Blessing Others

To bless means to wish, unconditionally from the deepest chamber of your heart, unrestricted good for others and events.

~ Pierre Pradervand

With each blessing you utter, your consciousness is raised and you help to raise the consciousness of those around you.

~ Eileen Cady

Blessing rituals are practiced in a variety of rites and ceremonies across cultures, and in some form in almost every religion, though not all blessings are faith-based. Blessings offered outside of a religious context are often less formal. "Do I have your blessing?" is a way of asking for permission and "I give you my blessing" can mean simply that a person is granting a request or embracing a new idea or procedure. It is said that the phrase, "God Bless you" originated with Pope Gregory during the Black Plague as a small prayer to protect someone from death. At some point in time, it morphed into "Bless you" being the polite thing to say when someone sneezes. Large numbers of people in cultures around the world bless the food they are about to eat and the hands that prepared it, and many who reject organized religion still say what is often referred to as grace before beginning a meal.

The Mezuzah hung on doorposts in Jewish homes pronounces blessings on those who dwell within as well as all who enter the house; other religions have various ways of blessing a new house and/ or the inhabitants of homes. There are also a multitude of rituals for blessing or cleansing one's home space conducted by any number of practitioners and guides from ceremonial artists to shamans to feng shui consultants.

Jesus exhorted his followers not only to love our enemies, but to bless those that curse us. In today's society, people often seem more likely to curse than to bless one another. Stuck in traffic jams for instance, we may observe drivers shouting at each other with clenched fists or raised fingers, or hear curse words flying through the air. We witness sports fans hurling curses at a player, a referee, or an umpire. We may pass people on the street swearing into their cell phones because they disagree with the voices on the other end. What a difference it might make if we all chose to bless instead of curse when such impulses arise.

Though many have grown used to relying on religious leaders to bestow blessings, in fact we all have the choice and the power to bless others if we have a pure intention to do so. Life presents us with myriad opportunities to practice the art of blessing. Blessings can take the form of supplication, praise, comfort, encouragement, or gratitude. A blessing can be vocalized, written, or silently sent as a meditative practice.

We can direct a blessing to a specific individual such as a child, grandchild or other loved one, to a parent, spouse, friend, neighbor, caregiver, teacher, or to a person who may have helped us in the past in some noteworthy way that we weren't aware of at the time. We need not wait for a designated day to bless our land, our forests, the fruit-bearing trees and vegetable gardens that nourish us, the earth on which we walk, and its natural resources which sustain us. We might put our attention on groups of people with the aim of directing a simple blessing or affirmation to them: newborn infants, traumatized children, struggling teenagers, children separated from their families unfairly, politicians, musicians, journalists, janitors, doctors, nurses, fire fighters, first responders, nursing home residents, victims of sexual assault, the disabled, the disenfranchised, the homeless, those who struggle with addiction or mental illness, those who are angry, depressed, living with chronic pain, or nearing death, the recently bereaved, and so on.

A blessing might be written on a sign waved during peaceful protests and marches for justice, or as a way of expressing appreciation for the heroes in our collective lives. We can use blessings to express gratitude for gifts of all types. We can bless someone for a simple kindness: the stranger who offers a helping hand when we're grappling with a heavy bag, the doctor who takes the time to sit down and listen to our fears as we struggle to adjust to a life-threatening diagnosis, or the vet who comes out to the car to euthanize a beloved animal companion in our arms instead of inside the building. We can bless someone for their courage, leadership, generosity, or support. "May you be blessed for all you are doing to help the poor in our community," or "Bless you for coming to help feed the hungry today."

This practice, much like my gratitude practice, began spontaneously. I can't pinpoint the specific date, though I remember that I was in the middle of a mental gratitude list when it seemed to naturally morph into sending blessings to the individuals or the groups that I was expressing gratitude for. Like any mindfulness exercise done regularly, sending out blessings is an activity that yields greater benefits over time. I have found that it is possible for us to bless those with whom we disagree, those we feel critical of, even those who may have mistreated or hurt us in the past. Although my birth mother died years before I took up this practice, I am able to feel gratitude for and bless her for giving birth to me, for letting me go instead of objecting when the judge made his pronouncement, and for her efforts to connect with me later in my life.

Major life challenges can turn out to be blessings in disguise. I am now able to regard as blessings unwished-for experiences such as my cancer diagnosis, which was daunting and scary at the time yet gave me exactly what I needed in terms of rest, resetting priorities, letting go of non-productive habits and behaviors, altering my diet and eating more mindfully. Rather than wishing events in my past had been different, or pretending something never happened, I choose to look at the past as being what has brought me to my life in the present. From that perspective, it is possible to view whatever may have occurred in our past as a blessing. The current Dalai Lama once said that if the Chinese government hadn't done what it did, he might never have had the opportunity to evolve his heart to be larger than the pain they brought.

Historically, blessings are often reinforced by a gesture such as uplifted arms or laying-on of hands. When we choose to bless someone, if the person is open to it, we might also physically touch that individual in some way which helps deepen our connection and reinforces the words we are saying. It could be an open hand over the person's heart, a hand laid gently on each shoulder, a firm handshake, or any kind of appropriate touch that is safe and which the individual is willing to receive. More than once, I have been greeted with a "Bless you" when I merely stopped to smile or say hello to an elderly resident sitting in an entryway or hallway of a care facility. Simple daily gestures such as a kiss on the cheek or placing one's hand for a moment on the head of a young child while saying "Have a good day," are essentially blessings, calling forth a wish for the safety and protection of a loved one.

Sending blessings to various individuals and groups of people eventually became a nighttime ritual for me as well a way to begin my day before getting out of bed in the morning, dovetailing with gratitude. Both practices are also useful when I find myself awake during the night and am having trouble getting back to sleep.

In a sense, we are also blessing others through any gesture of kindness or act of compassion we offer at any time in our daily lives. We have any number of choices to offering blessings in this way, from taking a meal to a friend in need to helping an elderly person get safely across a busy street. Blessings can be given in person, through the mail or sent out as a silent or spoken prayer. They can be transmitted through a song such as Bob Dylan's "Forever Young" or through a well-known hymn like "The Lord Bless You and Keep You."

The late Irish poet John O'Donohue writes about rediscovering our power to bless one another. In his book *To Bless the Space Between Us*, he defines a blessing as "a circle of light drawn around a person to protect, heal and strengthen," thus illuminating an individual or a situation in a new way. In his book, *The Gentle Art of Blessing*, Swiss author and sociologist Pierre Pradervand writes about blessing others as a way to "center ourselves in love." He believes that making a conscious choice to bless other people or beings around us can help make the world a better place. He observes that when we bless others, "without concern for their appearance, expression, race, class, sex, or any other label," it will expand our hearts. He also points out that it is impossible to bless and judge another at the same time and encourages us to hold fast to blessing as a sacred practice.

Fifteen

Forgiving

Forgiving is giving up the hope that the past could have been different.
True forgiveness is when you can say thank you for that experience.
~ Oprah Winfrey

Forgiveness is a way to set down old pain. It liberates us
from the wounds of our past . . . Sometimes we drive deep
into our wounds and come up with a precious gift.
~ Frank Ostaseski

Most major religions include teachings on forgiveness. Innumerable books have been written by psychologists, researchers, and religious leaders, as well as by everyday practitioners, that enumerate the psycho-social, emotional and spiritual benefits of forgiveness. The significance of forgiveness has been written about and extolled by modern-day activists and teachers from Mother Theresa to Nelson Mandela to Pema Chödrön. What all these individuals have communicated, in their own ways, is the importance of developing and maintaining our ability to forgive, how essential forgiveness is in any healing process, and that forgiveness is a path to liberation and inner peace.

Renowned peace activist Jack Kornfield, one of the key teachers of Buddhist mindfulness practice in the West, has shared several remarkable stories concerning forgiveness. He tells one about sitting with the Dalai Lama and a group of Tibetan nuns who were imprisoned during their teenage years for praying out loud and refusing to give up their religion. They subsequently survived years of captivity and torture. In a meeting with a group of ex-prisoners from the United States, along with the newly-released nuns, someone asked, "Were you ever afraid?" One of the women responded by saying that the thing they had feared most during their imprisonment was that they would succumb to hating their guards, that they would lose their compassion. The nuns reported that, while incarcerated, they had expressed their forgiveness for their captors through meditation practices. Another of the women in their group stated: "Just as we were incarcerated, our guards were not free. By doing their jobs and their duty, they were forced to be cruel."

When we have experienced traumatic injury or abuse in any form, we may never fully recover until we can forgive. My experience is that although forgiveness cannot be forced or feigned, it can manifest in a flash of new insight or awareness. It can also occur little by little as time goes by. Either way, forgiveness, whether of another or of ourselves, is a life-changing practice. When my birth mother appeared to me in such a surprising and intense way near the time of her death, and I kept repeating, "I forgive you," it was a response born out of compassion, without conscious effort. I felt some sort of release after the encounter. When the incident subsequently came up after that, I was emotionally detached when repeating it, thinking, naively, that the complicated relationship with the woman who gave birth to me had been sorted and settled.

After completing an assignment in a graduate school class entitled Transforming Grief, which required accessing a deep wounding in one's life and re-telling the story as myth, I was certain that I had forgiven her on a deeper level. Examining the archival documents that I received in the mail more than a decade later muddied the waters considerably, and threw me into an emotional tailspin. The new information exposed the depth of my mother's chronic neglect and rejection, forcing me to face feelings that I had no clue were still buried in my subconscious and in my body.

With persistence and determination, for the first time in my life, I was able to access and express those buried feelings emotionally and physically. As cathartic as that proved to be, there was an even deeper release to come.

It has long been my experience that a teacher in some form—a book, a quote, a situation, an individual—will appear when I one is ready to receive a teaching or shift to a deeper level of understanding.

While contemplating the meaning of forgiveness more deeply, I came across the YouTube video of the full Thich Nhat Hanh interview with Oprah Winfrey which can now be accessed. I had read several books by Thich Nhat Hanh, spent over an hour standing in a long line with hundreds of other people to enter an auditorium to hear him speak a number of years ago and had actually watched an edited version of his interview with Oprah when it took place in 2013, about a year and a half before Hanh suffered the stroke that limited his walking and speaking ability. And yet something was different this time. Perhaps I was mentally or emotionally more open or simply ready to receive his words in a new way.

In responding to a question Winfrey asked him about suffering, the eighty-five-year-old peace activist responded, "The first step in the art of transforming suffering is to come home to our suffering and recognize it . . . and the second step is for us to embrace it."

Those last few words were mind stopping. I hit a mental pause button and take a few deep breaths while letting the somewhat shocking idea of embracing, the seminal wound of my birth mother's abandonment percolate. Thich Nhat Hanh's countenance and his distinctive way of speaking, in that moment, opened my mind and heart as he introduced the idea that our bodies and our minds hold not only our own suffering, but also the unresolved suffering of our parents and of their parents, and so on, handed down from generation to generation, "because no one knew how to recognize, embrace, and heal it. It's not your fault, nor is it their fault."

The gentle sage then used an unusual term—"unskillfulness"—as something we all have in relating to others.

> The other person may not want to make us suffer or to hurt us. People can become victims of their own suffering. Without that understanding, forgiving is difficult. If you can understand the deep suffering in him or her, the situation becomes different. You can forgive more easily.

With great clarity and composure, he went on to say, "If we can heal our wounded child, we will not only liberate ourselves, but we will also help liberate whoever has hurt or abused us."

An extraordinary thing occurred for me as I listened to this benevolent monk, who had survived three wars, assassination attempts, and thirty-three years of exile, speaking with such certainty and compassion. His words simply **landed**. In that moment, I experienced an opening inside my being, a visceral feeling, as if some giant weight had been extracted. A sudden rush of energy filled me, along with what I could only describe as euphoria. I wanted to move, to dance, to sing, to thank and to praise the Divine. It was as if I had been shackled and was suddenly set free. I rose from my chair and began spontaneously moving around the space in ways I had not moved in years.

I open to my birth mother's suffering. She was undoubtedly wounded. She was suffering before she met my father, before I was born, and likely for her entire life. The choices she made grew out of the suffering of her mother and father and probably from their parents as well, contributing to intergenerational and unresolved trauma. She had been unable to heal the wounded child inside her. She was unskillful in the way she cared for me as a baby, and yet she was likely doing the best she could at the time. And it wasn't my fault. I was never not enough! I was never not worthy of love! I forgive her. I forgive myself . . . there is nothing to forgive.

In that timeless moment, I let go of the ghosts of the past. Whatever shards of blame I was still carrying in regard to the woman who gave birth to me simply dropped away, dematerialized, vanished. I became cognizant of the fact that, in subtle ways, I had been wishing I could have had a different mother, a different beginning to my life. Yet if my life had unfolded differently, I wouldn't be the same person I am today. Perhaps I was given the parents who facilitated my entrance into this world, and the exact experiences I needed in order to grow or evolve, to learn the lessons and experience the healing I took birth for.

The "story" about what occurred during my first year of life and other parts of my childhood is truly irrelevant. My thoughts about it are irrelevant. They don't have to keep taking up space inside my brain or my heart any longer. They only serve to keep me from being fully present in my life in the here and now.

A translated quote from the thirteenth century mystic and poet, Rumi, pierces my consciousness: "The wound is the place where the Light enters you." That perspective changes everything. Without the darkness, how would we find a path to the light? I feel as if I've been thrown through a portal into another dimension. Peace washes over me like a river.

The Healing Time

Finally on my way to yes
I bump into
all the places
where I said no
to my life
all the untended wounds
the red and purple scars
those hieroglyphs of pain
carved into my skin,
my bones,
those coded messages
that send me down
the wrong street
again and again
where I find them
the old wounds
the old misdirections
and I lift them
one by one
close to my heart
and I say holy, holy.

~ Pesha Joyce Gertler
(Pudding House Publications, 2008)

Appendix I

Last Visit with Nana

If you carry a memory of having felt safe with somebody long ago, the traces of that earlier affection can be reactivated in attuned relationships when you are an adult.

~ Bessel Van Der Kolk

The following is derived from a journal I was keeping in 1983 during the time of my last visit with Nana.

Nana is ninety years old/young. Her blue eyes are still clear and beautiful. She has moments of great lucidity when she knows who I am and speaks clearly and directly. She dozes off sometimes or makes a little humming sound. I find that sound inside of me, duplicating it, as I drift off to sleep at night. I read to her. We look at old photographs together. We create simple objects out of Play Dough. I tell Nana some of the things I remember her doing for me, and with me, through the years. I tell her how much I love her and how grateful I am for her unconditional love. Looking into my eyes, she says, "I'm so glad you're here." Then, shaking her right fist and index finger just in front of her smiling mouth in that way she often uses to emphasize an important thought, she says, "I do, do, do love you." I am so happy to be with her, to share, if only a little, in her process at this time in her life. Her body is so frail, I marvel that it keeps functioning. I can actually hear her food digesting and her heartbeat seems to almost shake her whole body. Sometimes we sit in silence, just being with each other. At one point, she says simply, without any judgement or emotion. "This is no way to be." I wonder what it is that keeps her hanging on to life in this physical form. When the live-in nurse makes her do something she doesn't particularly want to, she shakes her fork at her in mock anger. When she sees a picture of a baby or small child, her eyes twinkle and her face lights up as she smiles and smiles. When I show her a picture of herself, she opens her eyes wide, sticks her head forward and says, as if bemused, "Hello!"

I remain deeply thankful to have had those last sweet visits with my beloved grandmother wrapped in the warm cocoon of her deep and unequivocal love before she left her physical body behind. My appreciation for the significance of that gift in my early life and through adulthood continues to deepen. I wear the gold wedding band she wore for sixty-seven years and I've now worn for forty-three. She is with me always.

Appendix II

Practicing Gratitude

Gratitude is Heaven itself.

~ William Blake

Gratitude is not dependent on external circumstance.
It's like a setting or channel that we can switch to at
any moment no matter what's going on around us.

~ Joanna Macy

As Roshi Joan Halifax and others have expressed, "Gratitude is a state of mind." Turning to gratitude can calm and ground us when we're frustrated, frightened, anxious, confused, overwhelmed, grieving, or facing sudden, unexpected challenges. Choosing gratitude can help us refocus when we notice we are distracted. It can quiet our agitated minds. It can be cultivated until it becomes a habit, as routine and familiar as brushing our teeth or making our beds each morning. Practicing gratitude can be a consciously planned activity in and of itself, included in other daily rituals, or used as a simple, stand-alone meditative exercise. It can be useful as a way of " unwinding" or relaxing during a work break, after dropping children off at school, and at the end of a busy day. Listed below are just a few examples of when and where we might practice gratitude when by ourselves or as a shared activity with one or more other individuals.

- on waking in the morning before rising or when falling asleep at night

- at the beginning of any type of meditation practice or as a meditation by itself

- during a mindful walk in the park, while sitting in a public garden or on a beach

- lying on the grass looking up at a clear blue sky or at stars in the night sky

- while exercising at home, at a workout studio or in a gymnasium as a passenger in a car or on a bus or train or airplane

- when stuck in a traffic jam

- waiting in line at the post office, at the DMV, or at the grocery store

- waiting in an exam room with a dog or cat for the vet to arrive

- during halftime or intermission at a sporting or entertainment event

- walking up or down flights of stairs, riding in an elevator or on an escalator

- during a relaxing bubble bath or while taking a shower

- waiting to meet up with a friend or loved one at a designated venue

- during medical tests or anxiety producing hospital procedures

- before being rolled into the operating room for surgery

- sitting on the deck of a cruise ship looking out at the vastness of the ocean

Gratitude can be accomplished alone at any time in nearly any place. It might also be practiced with a friend, a neighbor, a partner, a parent, a spouse, a child or with any other companion or family member. It is a common and useful exercise in preparing us for a shared experience with a group of others before a meal, a meeting, a workshop, a meditation retreat or a Celebration of Life gathering for a deceased friend or relative. Gratitude can take the form of a prayer, a poem, a song, a meditation, a dance, or a painting. Our expressions of gratitude can be

- whispered

- shouted

- sung

- chanted to the beat of a drum

- repeated silently in our minds

- dictated on phone or computer

- hand written in a daily journal

- written on individual pieces of paper and dropped into a basket or bowl

- typed on a computer

- spoken over the phone, or emailed or during a zoom gathering by turns, with a friend or group.

- sent in a letter via postal service

- expressed in a group circle as a ritual

- collaged by oneself, with a partner, or in a group

- shared with a child or grandchild at bedtime

Try making a list of one hundred things you feel thankful for. If that seems like a daunting number, begin with ten things, and then let it expand naturally. You will be surprised at how quickly your list will grow the more often you engage in the exercise. If you are sharing the practice, simply take turns with the other individual, or with a small group until you reach an agreed upon number. For the sake of variety or expansion, try one of the variations suggested in the next section or choose one or two specific areas to focus on. One of my favorite exercises is to give thanks for individuals, or groups of people, who have helped or supported me in specific ways during my life thus far. I've been quite amazed at how far back in my lifetime (to even before I was born) that list has taken me.

During treatments for a life-threatening illness, while recovering from major surgery or from an immobilizing fall, gratitude takes on a whole new meaning.

- I'm grateful I have help and support from _____.

- I am thankful I can navigate the stairs in my house.

- I'm grateful I can walk to the bathroom toilet.

- I'm thankful for a cane (or crutch) to help me walk.

- I'm grateful I have time to watch the sunset.

- I'm thankful the hair on my head is coming back.

- I'm grateful my physical body is beginning to heal.

- I'm grateful I don't live alone.

- I'm thankful to be alive today.

- I'm grateful I feel well enough to go back to work.

- I am thankful I have good health insurance.

- I'm grateful I have a car and I can drive.

When we encounter challenging situations during a short-term or a chronic illness or infirmity, while undergoing difficult medical treatments, waiting for test results for ourselves or for loved ones, or while experiencing the emotional intensity of grief, pain, anger or sadness, it becomes important, even essential, to redirect our attention to what we can be thankful for.

A significant shift takes place when we focus our thoughts on the positive things in our lives rather than on the inevitable challenges that arise, on tasks we wish we didn't have to do, or on abilities we may have temporarily or permanently lost. A regular gratitude practice provides us with a stabilizing rudder as we navigate the river of uncertainty and change that is inevitable in our lives as human beings on this earth.

Try completing some form of a gratitude exercise, for whatever amount of time you choose, every day for one week or one month, or several months. Notice the difference it makes in your life. Keep doing the exercise when you are tempted to skip it. Experiment with practicing gratitude when you are feeling irritable, sad, or depressed. Try focusing on gratitude when you are experiencing emotional upset and/or you feel physical discomfort or pain anywhere in your body.

There are a variety of ways to engage in this practice which can be especially useful and enjoyable with an adult group or with children if you are a parent, grandparent or teacher. Below are some examples.

Alphabetical

I am grateful for . . .

Apples, apricots, asparagus, autumn, artichokes, avocados, athletics, airplanes, art . . .

Books, bagels, black beans, baseball, birds, babies, bridges, balloons, bubble-baths . . .

Candles, concerts, cafes, cinnamon, carrot cake, clothing, computers, cable cars, colors . . .

Down comforters, desks, ducks, drums, daisies, doctors, daylight, dreams . . .

Elastic, elephants, eggs, egrets, electricity, eyes, ears, escalators, exercise class . . .

Family, friends, flowers , forests, farms, fresh fruits, faucets, feet, fireflies, flannel . . .

Gardens, greenhouses giraffes, grapes, grapefruit, guitars, grocery stores . . .

Categorical

I am grateful I can use my body to . . .

 stand, walk, speak, clap, sing, chew, swallow, hug loved ones, drive a car, touch my toes, do the laundry, walk on the beach, prune the rose bushes, arrange flowers . . .

I'm thankful I can hear . . .

thunder cracking, birds chirping, rain falling, my cat purring, music playing, children laughing, a choir singing, a baby's cry, dogs barking, bells ringing, the phone beeping, my own voice . . .

I am grateful for light . . .

sunlight, moonlight, daylight, twilight, starlight, flash lights, brake lights . . .

I am grateful for the support in my life from . . .

family, friends, neighbors, book group, physical therapist, city services, handyman, plumber, pet sitter, postal workers, pharmacist, singing group, window cleaners, spiritual community . . .

I am thankful for water . . .

 bath water, drinking water, rain water, lakes, rivers, oceans, canals, melting snow, waterfalls . . .

Opposites

I am grateful for . . .

night and day, light and dark, hills and valleys, sun and rain, speaking and listening . . .

closeness and space, continuity and change, solitude and
companionship . . .

hot water and cold water, sunrises and sunsets, going out and
coming home, old and new, up and down, high and low, dawn and
dusk, inhale and exhale, laughter and tears . . .

big and small, above and below, young and old, giving and
receiving, buying and selling, empty and full, throwing and
catching . . .

Rhyming

I'm grateful for . . .

the garden, the flowers and the trees, the ocean, the fish and
especially the bees . . .

family, friends, those who care, for grandchildren, neighbors and
the bag of pears . . .

the sky, the moon, the stars at night, getting to the airport in time
for our flight . . .

soothing hot tea, books to read, a fireplace, watching my grand-
daughter complete a race . . .

the month of July, the azure sky, the tea they call chai, and this
fresh blueberry pie . . .

outdoors and indoors, carpeted floors, kitchen drawers, bookstores,
and s'mores . . .

Comprehensive

Alternatively, we can choose one thing, a loaf of bread for example,
and consider all the individuals who had a part in getting that bread
into our homes and hands: the farmer, the threshers, the bakers, the
packers, the truck drivers, the unpackers, the cashier, the baggers . . .

Mindful Gratitude

Not long ago I discovered an exhilarating and rewarding new way to combine Thich Nhat Hanh's conscious breathing technique and mindful focus on the present moment with gratitude. I was surprised at how easily it unfolded as my day began; and I was grateful for the undisturbed quiet that allowed me to focus in that particular way.

- Breathing in I'm grateful I can dress myself, breathing out I'm thankful for my body . . .

- Breathing in I'm grateful I can descend the stairs, breathing out I'm thankful for my legs . . .

- Breathing in I am grateful for this cup of delicious tea, breathing out I'm thankful for my hands . . .

- Breathing in I'm grateful for the sunshine, breathing out I'm thankful for flowers . . .

- Breathing in I'm grateful I can see, breathing out I'm thankful for autumn leaves . . .

- Breathing in I'm grateful for the rose bushes, breathing out I'm thankful I can smell . . .

- Breathing in I'm grateful for the teachers behind, around and within me, breathing out, I smile.

I happened to have an MRI (a type of test involving the use of magnetic and radio waves to produce images of the body's internal organs) scheduled for that same morning. The procedure requires lying on a lightly cushioned platform which moves one's body into a small tunnel-like tube. Unlike previous experiences with this particular exam, I was handed soft plugs to insert in my ears and what felt like two thick noise dampening pads were placed on either side of my head before I was sent into the tube with the instruction, "Do not move for the next twenty minutes." The sounds were just as loud as I remembered from earlier MRIs although they were not as rhythmic. I quickly returned to the practice I'd begun that morning. The regular rise and fall of my belly provided the rhythmic movement.

- Breathing in I'm grateful I'm not claustrophobic, breathing out, I'm deeply thankful to be alive . . .

- Breathing in I'm thankful for this test, breathing out I'm grateful we have health insurance. . .

- Breathing in I'm grateful I'm not tense, breathing out I'm thankful I can remain still . . .

- Breathing in I'm thankful for the compassionate technician, breathing out I'm grateful I can hear . . .

- Breathing in I'm grateful I'm able to relax, breathing out I'm thankful for this imaging technology . . .

Expanding the Practice

Country music singer and activist Willie Nelson, still performing in his nineties, once said that when he began counting his blessings his whole life turned around. Focusing our attention on the positive instead of the negative is a remarkably powerful practice. Gratitude can be an increasingly beneficial tool when we find ourselves distracted, flustered, depressed, disoriented or angry. Frank Ostaseski noted during an online workshop I participated in recently that it is difficult to be fearful or angry and grateful at the same time. A particularly good time to employ gratitude is when we are being challenged by a difficult situation or an unwanted responsibility; opening to our own or a loved ones' pain; the death of a close friend, family member, teacher, or student; the uncertainties of daily life; or simply the breaking news.

We can practice gratitude while adjusting to loss--of a close relationship, whether it be human, canine, feline or other species, or of a house, a dream, a business, a job. Another opportunity for cultivating gratitude arises when we are called upon to face something or do something we wish we didn't have to confront or undertake, whether that is moving to a smaller house, undergoing a lengthy surgery, getting up in the middle of the night with a sick child, saying goodbye to a friend near death or attending a memorial gathering or accepting election results. We can begin by finding one thing to be thankful for during whatever difficulty or challenge may be presenting itself. For example:

- I'm grateful I have an experienced physician I trust to perform my surgery . . .

- I am thankful to have known and loved _____ . . .

- I'm thankful I'm alive to honor my old colleague . . .

- I am grateful that I was able to give birth after having two miscarriages . . .

- I'm thankful I was able to say goodbye to _____ before she left her body. . .

- I'm thankful I am able to donate money (or time, or household items) to help those who have lost their homes and belongings in wildfires, floods, tornadoes, and other climate related disasters . . .

- I'm grateful for the opportunity to be a compassionate listener for another . . .

Yet another significant opportunity for practicing gratitude presents itself when we notice critical thoughts arising in our minds regarding a particular person or group. It could be an employer or employee, a spouse, a parent, a child, a friend, a neighbor, a political figure. The same opportunity arises when we feel perturbed or disgruntled by a situation whether it's stopped traffic, a long wait in an office, fast growing weeds in the garden, appointments cancelled at the last minute, a cranky toddler, an important vote that didn't go our way, unexpected inclement weather, or recovering from a surgical procedure.

- I am grateful I have a job that I enjoy . . .

- I'm thankful my adult children love and respect me . . .

- I'm grateful for shelter from the storms . . .

- I am thankful that the challenges of parenting are balanced by the rewards . . .

- I'm grateful I have friends who will listen to me without interrupting or judging me . . .

- I am thankful I can vote . . .

- I'm grateful I can still walk though I no longer run . . .

- I'm thankful I have enough energy to prune the rose bushes and pull weeds . . .

- I am grateful I have this opportunity to read a book without interruption . . .

When we are feeling frustrated, overwhelmed, sorry for ourselves, or annoyed with a particular individual or a situation in our lives, we always have the choice to put our attention on what we have to be thankful for within whatever may be pulling our minds into critical, negative or obstructive thoughts. It is possible to use gratitude as a tool in this particular way to shift our attention, expand our thinking, let go of negativity, set aside personal preferences, come to a workable compromise with a neighbor, a spouse or a child, to let go of our self judgements. Shifting our attention to what we have instead of what we don't have makes it much harder to continue feeling irritated or out of sorts.

- I'm thankful the roof of my house doesn't leak . . .

- I am grateful I have good health insurance . . .

- I'm grateful that my neighbor apologized for the loud music late last night . . .

- I am thankful I have been able to forgive _____ . . .

- I'm grateful for sunshine after stormy weather . . .

- I'm thankful for the physical therapist who is helping me
  with my back pain . . .

Oprah Winfrey once said: "If we are grateful for what we have, we will end up having more but if we continually concentrate on what we don't have, it will seem as if we never have enough." Every morning as I walk into our kitchen, I notice the small square of white paper with a few short lines in black just above the top of the built-in oven. I taped it there over twenty years ago. It is a quote by Meister Eckhart, the German theologian, philosopher and mystic, that continues to inspire me. The translation reads:

If the only prayer you said in your entire life is
Thank You, it would suffice.

Appendix III

A Forgiveness Practice

When we have experienced a deep injury,
we can never fully recover until we forgive.

~ Alan Paton (adapted)

It can sometimes be easier to forgive our enemies than our
friends. It can be hardest of all to forgive people we love.

~ Fred Rogers

We cannot force forgiveness. However, if we have the courage to open our hearts, it is possible for forgiveness to emerge. Many years ago, I attended a weekend workshop, with several dozen other people, led by the author and teacher Stephen Levine. At some point, he guided us through a powerful forgiveness meditation. The following exercise is adapted and expanded from Stephen's. The words can be read slowly and silently to yourself, or you may read them aloud to guide someone else through the practice.

Find a comfortable, quiet place to sit or to lie down where you won't be interrupted. Take a few moments to find a comfortable position . . . let your body relax . . . Bring your attention to your breath, slowly inhaling through your nose, then exhaling between slightly parted lips . . . Let your breath drop into your belly. Gently rest one hand on your abdomen, feeling it rise as you inhale and relax as you exhale a few more times . . . When you feel ready, let yourself begin to reflect on what the word forgiveness means, and more specifically what that word means to you . . . Notice any thoughts, words or images that arise in your mind . . . Notice any place in your physical body that may feel tense or tight in this moment . . . Inhale deeply and, as you exhale, visualize your breath going directly into that area of your body. You might want to give your breath a healing color such as pink or green as you send it . . . Open your mind . . . Open your heart . . . Take a deep breath, and slowly release the air through your lips as you exhale . . . Once again, inhale, exhale. As you continue to breathe normally, allow a name and/or a visual image of an individual whom you feel has treated you unfairly or unjustly arise, someone you are holding some degree of resentment or bitterness towards . . . See if you can allow an image or a sense of this particular person into your consciousness, into your heart, without forcing it. If you experience anger, fear, or anxiety arising, put your attention back on your breath for a few moments . . . Allow yourself to slowly, gently, soften just a bit around whatever feelings you may be experiencing . . . As an experiment, in this moment, without struggling or forcing, allow yourself to invite this person into your heart, just for a moment . . . Silently, in your heart, try saying to this individual, "I forgive you. I forgive you for the distress, the heartache, or the pain you have caused me, intentionally or unintentionally, through your actions or inaction, or through your words. In whatever way you may have caused me hurt or pain in the past, I forgive you." . . . Just for a moment right now, let yourself be open to the **possibility** of forgiveness, open to the possibility, however remote it may seem, of letting go of your anger or resentment toward this person so that you don't have to continue carrying that around with you. "I forgive you for whatever you may have done that caused me heartache or suffering, intentionally or unintentionally, through your actions, through your words, through whatever you did or didn't do. In whatever way the pain came to me through you, I forgive you. I forgive you." . . . In this moment, see if you are able to let go of the suffering your thoughts are causing you right now . . . Allow that person whose actions, intentional or not, caused you sorrow or distress, to be forgiven. Let your feelings of bitterness or rage or animosity slowly begin to dissolve. Let the space that person's actions are continuing to occupy in your heart and mind be freed . . . When you feel ready, allow that particular person's image to fade and disappear, touched by the possibility of your forgiveness . . . Notice how your physical body feels in this moment . . . And now, when you feel ready, take a deep breath. Slowly exhale. Inhale, exhale, relax. Inhale, exhale, relax . . . now gently bring into your mind and into your heart, the image of someone whom you sense might be holding resentment or anger towards you, someone whose heart may be closed to you . . . Invite that one into your heart and say, silently, or out loud, "I ask your forgiveness. I ask you to forgive me for whatever I may have done in the past that caused you pain or stress, intentionally or unintentionally, through my words or my actions. In whatever ways I may have hurt or injured you in the past, whatever I did that caused you anguish or unhappiness, I ask your forgiveness." Imagine yourself being forgiven . . . Have mercy on yourself . . . Allow that other to forgive you. Feel that forgiveness touching you. Let it into your heart. "I ask your forgiveness for however I may have caused you pain—through my anger, my fear, my ignorance or arrogance, through my frustration, my doubt, or my confusion. In whatever ways I may have caused you pain, I ask you for forgiveness." Allow yourself to be forgiven . . . If the mind attempts to block forgiveness with recriminations or self-criticism, just notice that and continue to breathe. Inhaling, exhaling. . . Let your mind and heart be touched by the possibility of being forgiven. Let your heart open to the heart of the other so that it may feel whole again. And now gently bid that person farewell. Without resentment or ill will, allow that person to be on their way, having even for a brief moment shared the one heart beyond the illusion and confusion of separateness . . . Inhale, exhale . . . Take a deep breath, inhaling slowly, and when you feel ready, exhale slowly . . . Now gently say, "I forgive you" to yourself. Open your heart to yourself. "I forgive you." Step outside the tyranny of self-judgement to forgive yourself. Use your name, and repeat silently or out loud, "I forgive you." If the critical mind intervenes, just notice those fixed thoughts, and allow yourself to soften even a little bit around them. Have compassion for your Self. Let yourself be touched by forgiveness. Let that forgiveness fill your body . . . Open to the warmth and care and compassion that wishes you well. Let your Self be loved. Embrace your Self. Be at peace.

With Gratitude To

. . . My husband Barry not only for helping me become a better writer and for editing my final drafts, but for listening to me, accepting me, encouraging me, walking with me through countless challenges and changes, co-parenting and co-grandparenting with me, supporting me in myriad ways and loving me since we first met over fifty years ago;

. . . Doug, for choosing me, loving me, helping me bring two incredible beings into this world, and for remaining my friend after neither of us was able to sustain the vows we had made, for encouraging me to marry again, and for co-parenting with us until his sudden, untimely death;

. . . Brianna, Michael and Meg, the three remarkable individuals whom I've been blessed to call my children in this lifetime, for pushing all my buttons, for being my greatest teachers, and for gifting me with your continuing love and adult friendship as you reach new goals, parent children of your own, and strive to make the world a better place;

. . . Katya and Stephan for our decades long extended family relationship across two generations, for fellowship, love and laughter shared, and for being laudable first responders in any crisis;

. . . Lawrence for over forty years of mentorship, guidance, and wise counsel, for his friendship, his inspiration, and for his unique and continuing contributions to my personal growth;

. . . Joanne for an ever growing and sustaining friendship since our young daughters brought us together over three decades ago, and for being someone I can always count on to celebrate, commiserate, laugh, or cry with me, or to simply listen;

. . . Cecily for reading countless drafts of my writing, for her unflagging enthusiasm and positivity, for her perceptive insights, generosity of spirit, and for always seeing the best in me;

. . . Carl and Marla, Goldie, Karen and other friends across the globe for their enthusiastic support in my writing endeavors, along with helpful ideas, and useful advice;

. . . Edrid, Anatta, Forest, Andy, Murray, Mark, Brock, Cynthia, Osha, Patsy, Anna, Edda, Tony, Willow, and other fellow seekers on the path who have paved the way, walked beside me, supported and/ or inspired me for over forty years and counting;

. . . Chavurah Alef, whose shared twice monthly pot luck Shabbat gatherings, special holidays, bat mitzvah celebrations and group Tikun O'lam projects enriched our lives for over a quarter century, giving rise to life-long friendships;

. . . My "Moms Over Forty" Support Group, drawn together by our decision nearly four decades ago to become mothers again or for the first time after the age of forty, for their wisdom, laughter, tears and memories shared;

. . . Author/teachers who have shaped and shaken my thinking, informed, and inspired me for decades: Pema Chödrön, Natalie Goldberg, Thich Nhat Hanh, Jack Kornfield, Stephen Levine, Frank Ostaseski, Helen Palmer, Ram Dass, Eckhart Tolle, Jon Kabat-Zinn, and more recently, Roshi Joan Halifax, Peter A. Levine, Gabor Maté, Jeffrey Rutstein, and Sharon Salzberg;

. . . Shelby Putnam Tupper and Carlos Wolters for their skill, generosity and support in helping bring this book to fruition.

~ a deep bow to you all ~

Suggested Reading

Chödrön, Pema, *Taking the Leap: Freeing Ourselves from Old Habits and Fears*, Boston, Massachusetts, Shambhala Publications, Inc., 2009.

Chödrön, Pema, *When Things Fall Apart: Heart Advice for Difficult Times*, Boston, Massachusetts, Shambhala Publications, Inc.1996.

Emmons, Dr. Robert A, *The Little Book of Gratitude: Create a life of happiness and wellbeing by giving thanks*, Great Britain, Gaia Books, 2016.

Gray, Enod, *Neglect—The Silent Abuser: How to Recognize and Heal from Childhood Neglect*, publisher unnamed, 1919.

Gil, Eliana, PhD, *Outgrowing the Pain: A Book for and About Adults Abused as Children*, NY, Dell Publishing, 1983.

Hanh, Thich Nhat, *No Mud No Lotus: The Art of Transforming Suffering*, Berkeley, California, Parallax Press, 2014.

Hanh, Thich Nhat, *RECONCILIATION: Healing the Inner Child*, Berkeley, California, Parallax Press, 2010.

Harris, Nadine Burke, M.D., *The Deepest Well: Healing the Long-Term Effects of Childhood Adversity*, NY, NY Houghton Mifflin Harcourt, 2018.

Hooks, Emily J., *The Power of Forgiveness: A Guide to Healing and Wholeness*, Forgiveness Academy, US, 2017.

Houston, Jean, *The Search for the Beloved: Journeys in Mythology and Sacred Psychology*, Los Angeles, CA, Jeremy P. Tarcher, Inc., 1987.

Kornfield, Jack, *A Path with Heart: A Guide Through the Perils and Promises of Spiritual Life,* NY, NY, A Bantam Book, Random House, Inc., 1993.

Levine, Peter A. with Ann Frederick, *Walking the Tiger: Healing Trauma,* Berkeley, California, North Atlantic Books, 1997.

Matousek, Mark, *Writing to Awaken: A Journey of Truth, Transformation & Self-Discovery,* Oakland, California, Reveal Press, 2017.

Meyers, Linda Joy: *The Power of Memoir, How to Write Your Healing Story,* Josey-Bass, SF, CA., 2010.

M.J. Ryan, ed. *A Grateful Heart: Daily blessing for the evening meal from Buddha to the Beatles,* Berkeley, California, Conari Press, 1994.

Noyes, Lawrence, *The Enlightenment Intensive: The Power of Dyad Communication for Self-Realization,* United Kingdom, Zenways Press, 2018.

O'Donohue, John, *To Bless the Space Between Us: A Book of Blessings,* NY, Doubleday, 2008

Ostaseski, Frank, *The Five Invitations: Discovering What Death Can Teach Us About Living Fully,* NY, NY, Flat Iron Books, 2017.

Pennebaker, James W. and Evans, John F., *Expressive Writing Words that Heal,* S. Bedford, IN, idyllarbor, 2014

Pradervand, Pierre, *The Gentle Art of Blessing: A Simple Practice that Will transform You and Your World,* NY, NY, Atria Paperback, 2009.

Rubano, Joseph P, *Go to the Edges: The Poetry of Joseph Rubano,* CA, True Meetings Press, 2017.

Salzberg, Sharon, *faith: Trusting Your Own Deepest Experience*, NY, Riverhead Books, 2002

Salbi, Zainab, *Freedom is an Inside job: Owning our Darkness and our Light Healing Ourselves and the World*, Boulder, Colorado, Sounds True, 2018.

Salzberg, Sharon, *The Kindness Handbook*, Boulder Colorado, Sounds True, 2015.

Taylor, Steve, *Out of the Darkness: From Turmoil to Transformation*, Carlsbad, California, Hay House, Inc., 2011.

Tolle, Eckhart, T*he Power of Now: A Guide to Spiritual Enlightenment*, Novato, California, New Old Library, 2004.

Van Derbur, Marilyn, *Miss America by Day: Lessons Learned from Ultimate Betrayals and Unconditional Love*, Oakhill Ridge Press, Denver, Colorado, 2003.

Van Der Kolk, Bessel, M.D., *The Body Keeps the Score*, Penguin Books, NY, NY, 2015.

Verma, Anu, *Victim 2 Victor*, Coventry, UK, England, Absolute Author Publishing House, 2020

Online Resources

There are a rapidly growing number of websites for identifying various sub-types of trauma from preverbal to adulthood, as well as suggestions and support for healing from specific forms of developmental trauma. Below are just a few I have personally found insightful or instructive.

Adult Survivors of Child Abuse (ASCA)
https://www.ascasupport.org

Center on the Developing Child Harvard University
https://developingchild.harvard.edu/science/key-concepts

Childhood Abuse and Neglect Stats
https://www.cdc.gov/child-abuse-neglect/about/

Childhood Emotional Neglect (CEN)
https://www.healthline.com/health/mental-health/childhood-emotional-neglect

Childhood Trauma and Depression
https://www.psychalive.org/link-between-childhood-trauma-and-depression

Effects of Childhood Trauma in first ten years of life on the decades that follow.
https://www.newportinstitute.com

EMDR Therapy
https://www.emdria.org/about-emdr-therapy

International Society for Traumatic Stress Studies
https://www.istss.org/home

https://www.parentingforbrain.com/childhood-emotional-neglect/

https://positivepsychology.com/childhood-trauma

About the Author

Dawn Nelson is the author of five books and co-producer of several award-winning videos. Completing a two-year graduate school certification course in "Awakening to Life and Death" in 1989-90 inspired Dawn to create the COMPASSIONATE TOUCH for Those in Later Life Stages™ program, which led to world-wide recognition as a speaker, author and touch educator. Dawn also has extensive experience in leading and helping facilitate three-day and longer residential meditation retreats as well as helping train others to give them. With the exception of an eight-month sojourn in Switzerland, Dawn and her husband have resided in the California Bay Area for close to fifty years. Now retired from teaching, Dawn continues to write, deepen her meditative practices and spend time as often as possible with her adult children, grandchildren, and several grand-dogs. She can be contacted through her website where you can read a number of her articles, access plenary talks, and more.

www.fromtheheart-hands.com

Index

A

abandoned 24, 28, 32, 106, 110, 111, 119, 152, 154, 172

abandonment iv, v, xiii, xv, xvi, xix, 3, 28, 101, 107, 121, 136, 189

abuse iii, v, xiii, xv, 3, 25, 110, 124, 188, 217

abusive iv, 35, 138

afraid 37, 44, 51, 57, 58, 75, 82, 118, 121, 154, 187

alcohol 18, 101

alcoholic 9, 13, 18, 104

alone xix, xxi, 12, 14, 15, 16, 17, 18, 19, 20, 24, 30, 34, 35, 36, 37, 42, 53, 58, 59, 61, 62, 74, 75, 76, 81, 82, 93, 94, 106, 110, 115, 116, 121, 131, 137, 146, 150, 152, 157, 171, 172, 195, 196, 198

angry 13, 31, 32, 37, 60, 76, 88, 93, 107, 110, 123, 138, 148, 154, 156, 170, 182, 203

anxiety xx, 33, 48, 54, 78, 79, 98, 153, 166, 175, 177, 196, 208

arguments 90, 92, 122, 123, 124

Arkansas 89, 95, 97, 98

ashamed 86, 92, 123, 136

attachment xv, 13, 140

aunt 28, 81, 83

Awakening xi, xiii, 129, 142, 143, 145, 219

B

baby xvi, 12, 15, 16, 18, 19, 20, 23, 52, 56, 57, 65, 71, 76, 88, 103, 105, 115, 116, 136, 170, 171, 173, 179, 190, 193, 200

beliefs 118, 134, 138

Bible 74, 110, 116

birth xvi, 3, 7, 9, 13, 15, 16, 19, 23, 34, 99, 101, 103, 105, 106, 110, 116, 125, 135, 136, 138, 142, 159, 170, 173, 178, 183, 188,

189, 190, 204

birth mother 15, 16, 23, 34,
99, 101, 135, 136, 138,
142, 178, 183, 188, 189,
190

blame xix, 37, 94, 172, 190

blessed 3, 142, 183, 211

blessing xiii, 181, 182, 183,
184, 185, 214

blood 72, 96, 115, 175, 177

brain xv, xvi, xix, 3, 13, 31, 41,
70, 110, 124, 137, 145,
150, 159, 166, 177, 191

C

cancer 105, 145, 176, 183

challenges 113, 143, 179, 183,
195, 199, 205, 211

childhood iii, iv, v, xiii, xv, xvi,
3, 21, 49, 77, 80, 109,
111, 123, 124, 125, 132,
138, 154, 169, 190, 217,
218

children iv, xvi, 3, 10, 24, 42,
45, 47, 49, 51, 62, 75, 80,
83, 84, 96, 103, 107, 112,
113, 116, 117, 118, 119,
120, 121, 132, 142, 159,
163, 164, 182, 195, 199,
200, 205, 211, 219

Pema Chödrön 97, 109, 187,
212

Christian 95, 98, 113

church 33, 74, 75, 89, 92, 94,
95, 98, 101, 102, 116,
117, 118, 162, 163

Cincinnati 5, 28, 38, 62

cognitive xv, 3, 52, 137

communication 85, 123, 131,
132

compassion iii, v, xv, 13, 16,
19, 49, 93, 105, 132, 150,
154, 157, 158, 176, 184,
188, 190, 209

conscience 41, 47, 51, 62

consequences 27, 109, 111

contact xvi, 99, 101, 107, 116,
132, 136, 141, 142, 150,
151, 152, 154, 157, 178

control 13, 33, 76, 91, 93,
110, 135, 151, 163

conversation 9, 70, 92, 99,
145, 150, 151, 164

cousins 74, 83, 84, 97

Peter Coyote 143

critical 15, 122, 136, 141, 183,
204, 205, 209

custody xxi, 10, 19, 21, 97

D

daily 50, 52, 59, 76, 110, 113, 132, 135, 151, 176, 177, 178, 184, 195, 197, 203

Dalai Lama 141, 183, 187

darkness 4, 19, 118, 171, 178, 191

deposition 11, 13, 15, 19, 20, 21

Depressed 12

depression xvi, xx, 13, 117, 124, 153, 154, 175, 217

developmental xiii, xv, 3, 169, 217

direct 142, 182

direction 69, 77, 145

directive 52, 54

distress 20, 26, 95, 125, 136, 169, 208

divorce 11, 28, 121

dog 69, 88, 95, 165, 196

drama 98, 111, 113, 178

dyad 131, 133, 134, 136, 137, 138, 140, 150

E

embracing 181, 189

emotional xiii, xv, xvi, xix, xx, 13, 30, 44, 49, 95, 100, 110, 116, 136, 142, 157, 159, 175, 176, 179, 187, 188, 198, 199, 217, 218

emotionally xix, 100, 112, 123, 124, 157, 188, 189

empathy 125, 154, 175

Enlightenment 129, 134, 138, 141, 142, 150, 214, 215

F

family iv, 26, 30, 31, 32, 54, 63, 65, 74, 82, 84, 86, 87, 88, 97, 105, 119, 121, 131, 149, 152, 154, 157, 164, 176, 177, 196, 200, 201, 203, 211

fear xvi, 3, 18, 33, 78, 112, 121, 158, 170, 208, 209

Florida 6, 7, 72, 101, 102, 103, 105, 178

forgive xv, 107, 123, 156, 163, 167, 187, 188, 189, 190, 206, 207, 208, 209

forgiveness iii, iv, 35, 187, 188, 189, 207, 208, 209

forgotten 24, 37, 49, 58, 74, 178

G

geographic dyslexia 77

good enough 4, 91, 110, 111, 135

grandchildren 3, 42, 165, 201, 219

grandfather iii, 11, 21, 22, 23, 45, 46, 64

grandmother 9, 16, 17, 19, 21, 23, 25, 26, 30, 31, 32, 34, 36, 44, 62, 64, 70, 194

grandparents ix, xxi, 9, 10, 14, 16, 21, 22, 26, 29, 31, 35, 36, 44, 65, 79, 97, 102

gratitude iii, iv, 19, 21, 36, 175, 176, 177, 178, 179, 180, 182, 183, 184, 195, 197, 198, 199, 202, 203, 204, 205

guilt 38, 71, 86, 106, 107, 117, 172

H

Joan Halifax 195, 212

Thich Nhat Hanh 5, 189, 202, 212

helpless 31, 33, 85

hospice 146, 147, 149, 151

hospital 17, 49, 50, 51, 54, 88, 105, 114, 115, 118, 146, 176, 179, 196

Jean Houston 169

husband 10, 26, 42, 52, 54, 62, 63, 71, 77, 84, 86, 99, 102, 103, 112, 113, 114, 116, 117, 118, 119, 120, 121, 122, 123, 135, 137, 140, 141, 145, 147, 148, 149, 151, 154, 211, 219

I

infancy v, xiii, xvi, 15, 26, 125

infant iii, xv, xix, 4, 19, 23, 107, 115, 170, 178

invisible 33, 37, 134, 137

J

Japan 140

M

married 26, 27, 29, 30, 73, 105, 112, 113, 119, 122, 124, 135

masterful 139

meditation xvi, 129, 140, 188, 195, 197, 207, 219

meditative 3, 95, 129, 132, 139, 141, 182, 195, 219

memory 4, 18, 21, 31, 34, 35, 36, 44, 46, 50, 58, 59, 61, 64, 81, 90, 105, 118, 193

mindfulness xvi, 183, 187

MOTHER xxi

music iv, 34, 71, 72, 74, 83, 93, 98, 149, 166, 177,

178, 200, 203, 205

N

Nebraska 98, 102
neglect iv, v, xv, xvi, 3, 16, 26,
    138, 178, 188, 217, 218
neglected xix, 24, 138
nervous 45, 69, 81, 101, 130,
    146, 163
newspaper 8, 15, 62, 63, 70,
    88, 98
Lawrence Noyes vii, xiii

O

John O'Donohue 184
ordeal 23, 79, 80, 103
Frank Ostaseski 145, 187, 203,
    212

P

pain v, 3, 4, 23, 32, 80, 115,
    117, 136, 146, 148, 166,
    170, 172, 182, 183, 187,
    191, 198, 199, 203, 206,
    208, 209
powerless 41, 69, 151
Pierre Pradervand 181, 184
prayer 62, 162, 181, 184, 197,
    206
preferences 137, 140, 143,
    152, 205

protected 4, 21, 69, 89, 115
punishment 58, 75, 80, 90

R

rape 109
reality 4, 94, 112, 133, 136,
    137, 143, 179
rejected xix, 24, 111, 138, 173
rejection xix, 4, 112, 122, 135,
    188
religious 96, 163, 181, 182,
    187
Rachel Naomi Remen 157
remorse 20, 117, 135, 172
rescued 17, 19, 24, 136
responsibility 13, 44, 80, 145,
    165, 203
retreat iii, 123, 129, 130, 131,
    132, 133, 138, 139, 197
Fred Rogers 132, 207
rules 95, 110, 130, 152

S

sad 32, 58, 107, 199
saddened 12, 86, 92, 153
sadness 13, 32, 49, 50, 90,
    124, 199
seen iv, xxi, 4, 32, 41, 44, 60,
    69, 75, 99, 107, 111, 120,
    123, 124, 134, 135, 139,

140

self-judgement 209

sexual 94, 109, 121, 130, 182

shame xvi, 86, 117

singing 74, 87, 117, 166, 200

spiritual iv, 58, 142, 143, 176, 179, 180, 187, 200

Benjamin Spock 80

subconscious 91, 110, 112, 138, 188

suffered 45, 148, 172, 189

suffering iii, v, 13, 24, 85, 132, 145, 154, 169, 189, 190, 208

suicidal 86

surrender 23, 141, 146, 157, 158

T

teacher 48, 64, 91, 92, 95, 98, 135, 178, 182, 188, 199, 203, 207

teaching 32, 46, 80, 116, 121, 134, 140, 145, 177, 188, 219

tears 20, 22, 26, 31, 47, 59, 77, 92, 107, 118, 123, 136, 167, 201, 212

telegram 84, 85, 103

testimony 17, 22

Texas 49, 50, 102, 113, 116, 117

theater 98, 112, 119, 123

therapist iv, 120, 163, 165, 178, 200, 206

therapy 3, 33, 146, 217

threat 43, 48, 137

threatening xx, 143, 183, 198

Robert Thurman 142

Eckhart Tolle 97, 142, 212

touch xiii, xvi, 44, 59, 103, 107, 123, 139, 147, 149, 150, 157, 158, 171, 177, 184, 200, 219

trauma iii, iv, v, ix, xv, xvi, xix, 11, 24, 33, 49, 61, 74, 109, 124, 125, 166, 169, 175, 190, 217, 218

truth v, 3, 53, 57, 63, 85, 89, 118, 129, 137, 139

U

uncle 74, 81, 83

uneasy 75, 81, 104, 130, 157

V

vulnerable 12, 33, 122, 154, 157, 158

W

wedding 8, 33, 34, 35, 73,

102, 107, 194

Oprah Winfrey 175, 187, 189, 206

wounded 190

wounds xvii, xx, 4, 157, 187, 191

For Reflection or Discussion

What made you decide to read this particular book?

Were their portions of the book that were difficult for you to
read and if so why?

Were there parts of the author's experience you
could relate to?

What feelings or emotions did reading the book
bring up for you?

Have you ever tried writing as a therapeutic exercise? If so
was it helpful?

Was there anything the author did not address in the book
that you wish she had?

What was the most important takeaway for you personally
from the author's story?

Notes